EXPLORATIONS IN JAPANESE SOCIOLINGUISTICS

Pragmatics & Beyond

An Interdisciplinary Series of Language Studies

VII:1

Leo Loveday

Explorations in Japanese Sociolinguistics

EXPLORATIONS IN
JAPANESE SOCIOLINGUISTICS

Leo Loveday
Doshisha University, Kyoto, Japan

JOHN BENJAMINS PUBLISHING COMPANY
AMSTERDAM/PHILADELPHIA

1986

Library of Congress Cataloging in Publication Data

Loveday, Leo.
  Explorations in Japanese sociolinguistics.

  (Pragmatics & beyond, ISSN 0166-6258; VII:1)
Bibliography: p.
1. Sociolinguistics -- Japan. I. Title. II. Series.
P40.45.J3L68   1986   401'.9'0952   86-26369
ISBN 90 272 2551 6 (European) / ISBN 1-556-19000-X (US) (alk. paper)

for my mother

FOREWORD AND ACKNOWLEDGEMENTS

The theme of this book is the interrelation of the Japanese language with its sociocultural setting and context: Japanese sociolinguistics. The study of language in Japan can provide the linguist with fruitful insights for theory construction as well as offering important data from a non-Indo-European language and a non-Western culture for comparative purposes.

For various reasons, some of which are discussed in chapter 1, information about this language and society has been neither sufficient nor accurate, myth and musing often interfering with characterizations. In the ensuing discussion, familiarity with Japanese is not presupposed and all examples appear in roman script. The first chapter and the second section of the last chapter utilizes only basic linguistic terms and their content is of a general nature so that they should be readily accessible to the non-specialist. The other chapters are, however, more technical: Chapter 2 is anthropologically oriented, following the school of 'the ethnography of speaking' while chapter 3 is heavily pragmatic in both theory and terminology and the first section of chapter 4 involves instrumental phonetics.

I believe sociolinguistics must adopt various disciplinary approaches in order to adequately analyse the multiple facets of real communication. Furthermore, the aim of much of the research presented here has not been primarily to explicate Japanese language behaviour so much as to exploit Japanese data to investigate or support a certain issue of wider, general significance. Thus, chapter 2 is an attempt to analyze the linguistic elements that feature in ritual activity (in any community), Chapter 3 examines the inadequacies of the structuralist paradigm and both sections of chapter 4 demonstrate the conflict arising out of differences in communication patterns across cultures.

However, it is hoped that this volume will contribute to a firmer and more theoretical appreciation of the linguistic and social dynamics of the Japanese speech community. In particular, chapter 1 offers an extensive survey of the field of Japanese sociolinguistics which may serve as a source of reference to newcomers to the field as well as providing a broader framework in which to consider the arguments of the subsequent chapters.

Some of the material presented here has previously appeared as separate articles in various journals and books and I particularly wish to thank the following editors and their publishers for permitting it to be reprinted again: Professor Voeglin, editor of *Anthropological Linguistics* which originally published "Making an occasion: the linguistic components of ritual" (in Vol. 23, No.4, 1981); Professor Enninger (with M. Lilith) who edited *Studies in Language Ecology* (Wiesbaden: Franz Steiner, 1984), in which "The ecology of designatory markers" appeared and who was co-editor (with R.J. Brunt) of *Interdisciplinary Perspectives at Cross-Cultural Communication* (Aachener Studien zur Semiotik und Kommunikationsforschung, Bd.2; Aachen: Rader, 1985) which first published "At cross-purposes: semiotic schism in Japanese-Western interaction"; Professor Sigurd of *Studia Linguistica* which published "Japanese donatory forms: their implicatons for linguistic theory" (in Vol.36, Part 1, 1982); Professor Abramson of *Language and Speech* where "Pitch, politeness and sexual role" first appeared (in Vol.24, 1981) and Professor Jacob Mey who invited me to write an introductory survey of Japanese sociolinguistics for a special issue of *Journal of Pragmatics* appearing in 1986.

It has long been my ambition to be able to collect these scattered papers and offer them as one volume and I am extremely grateful to Professor Herman Parret and Professor Jef Verschueren as well as John Benjamins for their encouragement and advice in this matter.

Kyoto 1986

TABLE OF CONTENTS

LIST OF FIGURES, TABLES, DIAGRAMS

1. JAPANESE SOCIOLINGUISTICS - WITH SPECIAL REFERENCE TO WESTERN RESEARCH

1.1. Japanese language and society

The Japanese language has developed and is embedded in a particular social and cultural system and the purpose here is to relate these two in a comprehensive yet succinct and accessible manner for those unfamiliar with either. Due to the difficulties of approaching the matter in this way, certain simplifications and overgeneralizations are inevitable, although I have tried to avoid them. The majority of research reviewed here has been especially selected because it has been conducted by non-Japanese researchers and therefore fuller explanations are usually available in English (or sometimes German). However, the work of Japanese investigators will also be mentioned when their work is in English or, if not, particularly relevant and significant. Western researchers frequently offer different insights and follow different approaches from native scholars (cf. section 1.2. below). Until only very recently the literature in English on Japanese sociolinguistics was very limited and there were few non-Japanese researchers. Today, it is encouraging to observe the contemporary increase in studies by non-Japanese which reflects the growing internationalization of the field of Japanese sociolinguistics.

1.1.1. *Japan-related speech-communities*

The term 'speech community' implies neither a particular size nor any particular basis of communality (cf. Fishman 1969: 22) but its existence results from its members' sharing of a single speech variety together with the norms for its appropriate use. The nation of 119 million Japanese reveals a remarkable degree of linguistic homogeneity with Japanese spoken as the mother tongue of almost all its citizens (apart from the handful of those naturalized). Literacy is officially declared to be 99%[1] which underlines the uniformity (desired) in this community.

Although linguistic minorities are demographically insignificant and no provisions are made for them by the authorities, it is nevertheless wrong to

accept the widely propagated myth that "Japan is a monolingual, monocul-
tural and monoethnic country ... (and that) we have no problems concerning
... languages in contact, ethnic troubles in language and bilingualism or linguistic minorities" as Shibata (1985: 88) announces to be the case (cf. sections
1.5.1. and 1.5.3. for aspects of language contact and bilingualism in contemporary Japan).

Admittedly, the number of Ainu[2] speakers is now so tiny that language
death appears inevitable before the end of this century due to the decline of
the community through intermarriage and ethnic identity reorientation to
Japaneseness. 15,000 Ainu are estimated to be living in Hokkaido and a
further 1,500 on Sakhalin. The minority status of Okinawans has never been
officially recognized and their linguistic variety is falsely subcategorized as a
Japanese dialect (cf. note 23 and p.12). A more sharply differentiated ethnic
minority are the Koreans who number 670,000 (of whom 101,000 were born
in Korea and 50,000 educated at local ethnic schools in Japan). In addition to
the Koreans there are 45,000 Taiwan Chinese and another 20,000 Mainland
Chinese. International refugees number 5,200 and include 2,820 Viet-
namese. According to the Justice Ministry's Immigration Department there
were 933,000 foreign residents[3] altogether in Japan with 700,100 of these per-
manent in 1984.

Furthermore, various types of Japanese-speaking communities exist
OUTSIDE the country such as:
(1) temporarily resident Japanese businessmen and their families (and
accompanying personnel infrastructure) in all the major economic centers of
the world whose bi- and multilingual/-cultural children increasingly challenge
the popular monolithic stereotype of monolingualism on their return to Japan
(cf. section 1.5.3.);
(2) established immigrant communities in North and South America and
Hawaii[4] (cf. section 5.3.) some of which date back over a century and which
typically involve language shift away from Japanese to a dominant language
such as English or Brazilian Portuguese;
(3) older generations in Korea and Taiwan who under Japanese colonial
domination[5] experienced education and the conduct of their country's public
affairs in Japanese until the termination of World War II form an ageing
group of overseas second-language Japanese speakers.

1.1.2. *The Japanese language*[6]

Japanese is a SUBJECT-OBJECT-VERB language, often labelled as
agglutinative. It is noted for its postpositions, noun classifiers and honorific

system. Its phonological structure is basically CONSONANT + VOWEL with open syllables, but contact with Chinese (cf. section 1.5. below) has led to the development of double consonants and a nasal in final position. It is also a syllable-timed language whose words contain an inherent tone pattern that occasionally can be distinctive. The indigenous Japanese vocabulary consists predominantly of two- or three-syllable words but wide borrowing from foreign languages has led to longer forms. Native taxonomies for fishing, rice cultivation, plants, weather, social relations and positions are particularly extensive (cf. Lewin 1981: 1795).

A standard (spoken and written) language based on the speech of the capital Tokyo is widely understoood and employed today although there are also many local dialects (cf. 1.3.1.)

The origin of Japanese has been the subject of much controversy and speculation since linguistic evidence remains too scanty for definite statements. It seems to share certain features of its neighbours which has led to its identification with Korean, Altaic, Malayo-Polynesian, Tibeto-Burmese and even Dravidian. These posited links suggest that it may have developed originally as a contact variety. Japanese is not related to Chinese even though 47% of its lexicon is made up of Chinese loans and its orthographic systems derive from Chinese characters[7].

Various systems for transcribing Japanese in roman script have been devised but here the Hepburn system is employed since it offers a close phonetic rendering of Japanese[8].

1.1.3. *Japanese sociolinguistics as a field of study*

Of course, the discipline of 'sociolinguistics' itself has only formally emerged since the early sixties. As Japanese academics do not usually concern themselves with innovatory paradigms, preferring instead the established and traditional, it is not surprising that Western sociolinguistic theory is only now beginning to be widely appreciated. One major problem here is the separation between national language scholars (*kokugogakusha*) who do not generally expose themselves to Western theories and linguists (*gengogakusha*) who rarely study their own language and specialize in European languages, usually English[9]. As well as isolationist attitudes, Grootaers (1967) mentions the persistence of feudalistic structures in which professors stifle independent research and hierarchical organization based on seniority fostering hostility towards new theoretical approaches.

On the other hand, it has to be noted that 'national language scholars' have long recognised the social and cultural embedding of their language[10].

Furthermore, they had developed an indigenous form of sociological dialectology termed 'language life' (*gengo seikatsu*) as early as the 1940's. This field has been closely associated with the Japanese National Language Research Institute which has produced descriptive surveys mainly concentrating on particular regional varieties with a statistical orientation[11]. This survey approach culminated in the publication of the "Linguistic Atlas of Japan" (1955-1975) which basically presents maps depicting regional variations on individual lexical items. There has been a shift over the years from methodology and general surveys of communities to the study of politeness levels (honorifics), dialects in contact, sex differences in language and children's speech (cf. Grootaers and Shibata 1982; Shibata 1985).

Shibata (1975) introduces some prominent sociolinguistic topics in Japan such as honorifics, borrowing and language standardization as a contribution to the only English book so far to be entirely devoted to Japanese sociolinguistics and entitled "Language in Japanese Society" (Peng (ed.) 1975). This collection of articles is divided into four sections: the description of non-standard varieties, kinship behaviour and the use of pronouns, language attitudes and foreign language learning. Some of this work, of which a large portion is statistical and linguistically difficult for non-Japanese specialists, will be mentioned below.

Until now Japanese sociolinguistics has tended to focus heavily on data and statistics. The one exception is the usually short essay dealing with Japanese language and culture in a very loose and general way. It is obvious that a stricter theoretical focus with a closer incorporation of Western concepts and terms will not emerge until younger researchers, exposed and trained in sociolinguistics, assume leading positions in Japanese universities.

1.2. Encoding social organization

This section will present research available in English pertaining to the way the Japanese language reflects social structure, behaviour and patterns of affiliation. Only a brief, introductory outline of the issues is offered since this paper is intended for those with little background knowledge.

1.2.1. *Verbal honorifics*

One of the most widely reported sociolinguistic components of Japanese is the honorific system of which only its verbal aspects will be dealt with here[12] (cf. also Martin 1964, O'Neill 1966, Miller 1971, Martin 1975: 331-354, Goldstein and Tamura 1975: 96-121 and Ide 1982).

There are two dimensions to honorific verb forms in Japanese: REFE-RENT HONORIFICS which, from the most simplistic view, 'honour' a specific person and his actions and belongings as well as persons affiliated to him, and ADDRESSEE HONORIFICS which, again simplistically, 'hon-our' a person to whom the speaker is talking. Of course, it is often the case that the referent honorificated in an utterance turns out to be the addressee but it is important not to confuse the quite distinct devices.

Japanese verbal referent honorifics are divided into subject honorifica-tion (*sonkeigo*; cf. Harada 1975: 816) which exalt the subject of a sentence[13] and object honorification (*kenjō-go*) which elevate the object and deprecate the subject and is used to express respect more intensely[14].

Furthermore, there are two social levels for addressee honorifics which symbolize respect to the interlocutor: polite addressee honorifics and, for greater deference, exalting addressee honorifics[15]. Finally, it must be added that both referent and addressee honorifics can combine in various ways for particular effects[16].

Martin (1964) claims that four factors determine the choice for hon-orifics: social position, age differences, sex differences and outgroupness. With reference to the latter, Nakane (1974) claims that there are three clear categories of interpersonal communication for the Japanese: (i) those people within one's own group (ii) those whose own background is fairly well-known to the interactant and (iii) those who are unknown strangers. Honorifics often occur in the first two contexts where hierarchical relations are involved; the distance in the third situation does not automatically lead to polite forms but often informality and even rudeness[17]. However, even in the intimate circle, honorific forms are expected to be used by inferiors to superiors in terms of age or status (cf. also Nakane's (1970) depiction of Japanese society as so ver-tically structured that members find it impossible to operate horizontally).

Nevertheless, it would be mistaken to understand honorifics as mere markers of inferiority/superiority since they are also employed to mark fictive statuses[18]. These fictive statuses may be alluded to for a variety of as yet not fully explored reasons such as to highlight sexual differences (Miller 1967: 289; cf. 3.2.1.), to express formality because of setting constraints (Neus-tupny 1978: 220 and 222) or to create or level social distance, mark the addressee as either belonging in or outside one's group, for stylistic purposes such as sarcasm, raillery and humour (Shinoda 1981), to support face, to seek favour or patronage (Mio 1958), present specific messages such as expressing gratitude, to protect individual space and privacy (Ide 1982), to "decorate" exchanges of business and service or to indicate the "cultural refinement" of the speaker. In fact, the findings of the sociolinguistic survey into honorific usage in Tokyo conducted by Ogino et al. (1985) demonstrate a close correlation between the frequency of honorifics and variables such as femaleness, adulthood, higher education and white-collar occupations such as professionals, administrators, office workers and shopkeepers, which suggests that honorifics play an important role as social class markers.

It appears that addressee honorifics, particularly among the urban, are increasing while at the same time the system is growing more complex as the number of forms and styles proliferate (cf. Miller 1971).

1.2.2. *Terms of reference and address*

In Japanese various linguistic means are available to refer to or address a person such as pronouns, kin/role terms and suffixes (a simple flow chart of the suffix patterns used in address appears in Fig.1). Included in these are elevatory and deferential forms which are traditionally viewed as part of the honorific system. The fact that Japanese has many 'I' and 'you' words has been widely reported but, in fact, they are more frequently avoided then employed, particularly in the case of third person pronouns (cf. Hinds 1975)[19]. Russel's (1981) research on the use of second person pronouns among college students reveals that men and women usually use the first name, nickname, or last name or kinship or occupational title in second person reference. Voeglin and Yamamoto (1977) discuss the difficulty of appropriately interpreting the meaning of first and second pronouns due to deixis and their multiple values, e.g. women use the second person pronoun *kimi* 'you' only with intimates or those of inferior status, but men may use it when speaking to strangers.

Ishikawa et al. (1981) provide the most comprehensive account so far of Japanese address terms as a system with a highly complex flow chart which involves six categories: kin terms, first and last names, professional names (e.g. 'teacher'), post-designating terms (e.g. 'section chief'), second person pronouns and fictives[20]. These authors note how the address system reflects "the hierarchical characterization of relationships as higher and lower with regard to age, sex and role ... (with) power semantics as its most fundamental property" (1981: 139). Pronouns appear only appropriate to persons of equal or lower rank.

Goldstein and Tamura (1975) present a clear introduction to Japanese kin terms. Comparing them with those of English, they find that unlike the

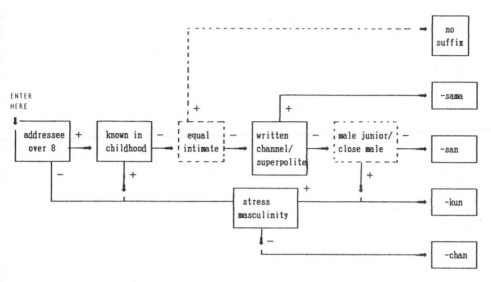

Fig. 1. FLOWCHART OF JAPANESE SUFFIXES OF ADDRESS AND REFERENCE. (The dotted lines and boxes are only to be entered when a male is addressing another male). This is only an abstract formalization of the general patterns. A speaker might well proceed to -san in every case. What is discernible is how significant ranking on the basis of age (-kun/-chan), sex (-kun, -san, no suffix) and superiority/inferiority (-kun, -san, -sama) features, all of which are fundamental themes of Japanese social organization.

Japanese, in the American family outside the categories of parents and grandparents, all other relatives are addressed by name and the names of siblings make no age or sex distinctions. In Japanese there are terms to refer to one's family group when speaking to outsiders of the family[21]. These features "are a fundamental part of a linguistic world that cuts off one's own family group from others and later cuts off other important groups in a similar way" (1975: 57).

In an earlier but fuller discussion of Japanese kinship terminology, Befu and Norbeck (1958) observe that the choice of alternate terms and variants of kin terms depends upon the operation of a number of factors such as relative social status, degree of intimacy of interactants, patterns of authority applying between relatives, and the formality of the occasion. Furthermore, Peng's (1975) investigation into the sociolinguistic patterns of Japanese kinship behaviour among junior high school students concluded that sex, age, householder's vocation (e.g. farmer) and attitudes towards communicative distance were significant variables in the employment of kin terms. Further studies on this topic available in English are Tanaka's (1977) account of Okinawan kinship terminology and Prindle's (1972) rigorous structural and historical analysis of Japanese consanguineal kin terms.

Finally, it should be mentioned that terms of address and reference should not be thought of as limited to pronouns, titles, name suffixes or honorific verbal devices. There exist, for example, a set of five lexemes[22] in Japanese which correspond to the one English verb 'give' (cf. chapter 3). These donatory verbs clearly indicate group affiliations, social positions and other aspects of interpersonal relations; they occur frequently in requests and orders, often being employed in cases where Western languages would use pronouns. All in all, the area of Japanese terms of address and reference seems to have undergone extensive research and a considerable amount of information is available on the subject.

1.3. Social Variation

1.3.1. *Standard and regional varieties*

Neustupný (1974: 36) succinctly characterizes the contemporary situation regarding varieties: "The spread of the modern Japanese standard as a means of both written and spoken national language has been remarkably successfull. It is true that the dialects survive as native varieties of a large number of speakers, but for all speakers the school-acquired standard is superposed".

Every member of the Japanese speech community can understand the written and spoken standard variety which has been spread by centralized, compulsory education, mass media, levelling and mixing processes in the Second World War and, more recently, urbanization (cf. Lewin 1979; for the historical development of the standard in relation to language planning cf.1.4.1.). However, as Grootaers (1982) notes, in the family the local dialect is retained, especially on the phonological and grammatical levels. Grootaers (1967) provides a summary of the century-old research on Japanese dialects together with a detailed bibliography including work in English. The research has been conducted mainly as statistically-based surveys on particular locations and produced maps depicting regional variations in lexical items (Linguistic Atlas of Japan, 1955-1975). Furthermore, the tonal differences between dialects have been widely explored and even a few dialectal grammars produced while dialectal dictionaries have tended to focus on the 'exotically' different vocabulary from the standard.

The Japanese speech community is made up of many persisting local dialects, although fear for their survival is often voiced (some of which are mutually unintelligible) as well as the officially supported and promulgated standard (*hyōjungo*). The latter represents the systematization of the speech of the 19th century educated élite (originally samurai bureaucrats) in the Tokyo area and the incorporation of certain expressions from the nobility who accompanied the Emperor Meiji when the capital was transferred to Tokyo (after the Restoration of 1868) from Kyoto whose dialects had provided the basis for classical Japanese for more than 1,000 years.

Nomoto (1975) discusses the standardization process by examining statistical data gathered with a 20 year interim and predictably finds that younger speakers and those with higher levels of education evidence greater susceptibility to standardization, with the latter being the more significant factor. From the National Language Research Institute's surveys it would appear that the most important variables for the presence of dialectal features are age, parents' origin (particularly mother's), speaker's profession (independent professions tending to employ more dialect) with sex and other social differences proving insignificant (cf. Grootaers and Shibata 1982: 349). An interesting influence on dialect acquisition seems to be school location so that members of the same family who attended different primary schools sometimes reveal varying usage for a few lexical items.

Japanese dialects have been classified in various ways. However, the labelling of the Okinawan variety as a Japanese dialect is controversial[23] because, if so classified, it means that the Okinawans are assigned a Japanese ethnicity which is not acceptable to all Japanese nor Okinawans. The Ryūkū islands were a politically separate kingdom up to the beginning of the 17th century and maintained internal autonomy[24] until the end of the 19th century when the monarchy was abolished and it became a Japanese prefecture. Today young Okinawans only know standard Japanese due to rigirous educational suppression in the past of the Okinawan variety, which now faces extinction inspite of local attempts to revive it.

As for mainland dialects, these are usually divided into Eastern, Western and Kyūshū or simply split into Eastern and Western groups, the latter including Kyūshū. The Tokyo dialect belongs to the Eastern group but has become increasingly westernized during the last two centuries and does not differ radically from that of Kyoto except for word tones and a limited number of other features. The Kyoto variety continues to enjoy a certain prestige due to its position as former imperial capital and home of traditional culture. It is associated with the linguistic styles of entertainers such as the geisha and kabuki actors, craftsmen such as kimono makers and the art schools of ikebana. However, young Kyotoites appear to be shifting towards the more modern appeal of the variety of the major economic Western centre, Osaka, which is associated with young styles promoted by the media and a genre of comedy frequent on TV (*manzai*).

Japanese researchers have rarely investigated the spectrum of attitudes to dialects or the standard. Yamagawa's (1967) paper is essentially on dialect intelligibility although attitudes are briefly touched on. As for the former situation, an experiment revealed that regardless of their place or origin or place of longest residence, the majority of informants showed a sound understanding of the dialect of the former capital, Kyoto, and other dialects of the "heartland" such as the Kantō area through Aichi, the Kinki district, the Inland sea, Kōchi and Kumamoto. Yamagawa attributes this to the fact that this is the area in which industry, commerce and transportation have most strongly developed and where most political and legal activity is centered as well as being the location of major educational institutions. Least intelligible were the dialects of the deep North and deep South such as Tōyama, Nagano and Kagoshima i.e. the least developed economic areas.

Perhaps more interesting is the "representative" range of opinions expressed by students taking part in Yamagawa's experiment which express both sentimentality and negative prejudice: "the dialects are full of local colour and very attractive. When I listen to the speech of the provinces I am so happy that I weep. How I long to hear them" (1967: 12); "I was really surprised to learn that there were so many dialects in such a small country as ours. Unless the government works to have the standard language more completely adopted the country will not prosper" (1967: 12).

Today, certain feelings of inferiority characterize strong dialect speakers in the face of standard users who are not members of their own regional community which is a reflection of the widespread, acknowledged prestige of the standard. However, covert dialect prestige among members of the same community exists but has yet to be investigated as do many other sociolinguistic dimensions of Japanese dialects such as situational code-switching between regional and standard varieties, the influence of mass media as model and presenter of varieties, language planning and education in the standard, the effects of university education on the speech-style of students from different regions who acquire new varieties and the social expansion of dialects other than the standard such as that of Osaka.

1.3.1.1. *Oral and written varieties*

Up until the end of the Second World War Japan was a diglossic society when it came to the employment of the written variety, especially for official communication (cf. Müller 1975). Even certain oral styles were not intelligible to ordinary community members. A famous example is the case of the Emperor's radio speech (1945) calling for surrender at the end of the war which was not understood by most listeners and even misinterpreted by others as a declaration of victory.

This High variety relied heavily on classical Chinese structures and phraseology which formed the basis for all formal Japanese writing up until the end of the 19th century (cf. 1.4.1.). In fact, during the period of adopting the Chinese writing system from the 5th century onwards until the emergence of established notations for the Japanese language in the 9th century, there was a diglossic bilingual situation with regard to writing so that the Chinese language was generally employed for administrative, academic, religious and literary texts[25]. This Chinese legacy permeated classical Japanese and formal written styles until the middle of this century[26]. From the end of the 19th century, however, the gap between oral and written varieties started to narrow as a result of experimental literature (cf.1.4.1.).

Today, a closer correspondence between oral and written varieties is being attempted in certain types of popular publications (cf. Osawa 1977). Traditionally, written-style sentence endings are usually nouns while oral Japanese ends with various forms including verbs and adverbs too. "Written Japanese and spoken Japanese are still in disagreement as to the direction modern Japanese will take" (1977: 254).

Finally, it should be noted that the oralization of the standard such as for news reporting on state media (NHK) is still felt to be 'unreal' and 'artificial' which shows that the speech community has not yet fully adopted the official, oral standard model for its own use unlike that of the written.

1.3.2. Identity markers

In Japan, it is often possible to detect social features of identity in a written text e.g. in the selection of lexis, sentence endings and the calligraphy. However, a sociology of Japanese writing has yet to be produced. This section briefly reviews areas in which Japanese may consciously or unconsciously produce and perceive social information related to age, gender and group identity in their communication. Of course, regional identification is frequently possible on the phonetic, phonological and suprasegmental level, particularly in word tones, even when the speaker employs standard grammar and vocabulary.

It should be remembered, on the other hand, that there is not always a simple, one-to-one correlation between identity markers and linguistic symbols but that the former dynamically emerge in the course of interaction and through awareness of a particular social context (cf. Brown and Levinson 1979: 292).

1.3.2.1. *Gender*

The relationship between gender and language is probably one of the most extensively reported fields in Japanese sociolinguistics. Various sex-based linguistic distinctions are already observable in the classical literature of the Heian period (794-1192) when women were not permitted to write Chinese characters but restricted to the syllabic system, which prevented their access and contribution to higher, intellectual levels of the written channel. The notion that males and females belong to different spheres has long prevailed among the upper class and is encapsulated in the proverb: *onna wa onna dōshi* (lit. 'women with fellow-women') and this has filtered down to the historically more egalitarian-thinking, lower classes over the ages. Women have long been accorded a lower status than men and until the Second World War were expected to show "deference to men of their own as well as higher classes through the use of polite language and honorific forms of address, bowing more deeply than men, walking behind their husbands in public and in numerous other ways deferring to men" (Pharr 1976: 306)[27].

However, an explanation of the contemporary linguistic behaviour of females in Japan which is generally much politer than males should dwell less on status difference and more on role-fulfillment obligation. As Lakoff (1975) pointed out for Western women, females are expected to be decorative in the way they dress *and talk*. The occurrence of high politeness forms in Japanese female speech should be similarly interpreted as the symbolization of femininity as well as social inferiority. Furthermore, in contrast to the West, it would seem that, in Japan, conformity to socio-behavioural norms is taken as more fully constituting the sexual identity of a person than psychological traits cf. Lebra's (1974: 87) comment: "sexuality for the Japanese seems foremost a role concept".

Most research in this field has focussed on sex-linked use of pronouns and sentence-final particles but it is important to realize that gender expresses itself on multiple linguistic levels. For instance, on the phonetic level of the pitch correlates of politeness (cf. chapter 4 of this volume), Loveday found that Japanese female subjects adopted a falsetto mode while males took a low profile. This contrasted with the performance of English informants of both sexes whose pitch levels were less differentiated, suggesting that the Japanese sex-role expectations are more rigid than those prescribed by English norms. In this connection it is interesting to consider the comments of Cammack and van Buren (1967) concerning Japanese female voice quality, the features of which are breathiness, openness, and lowered volume in comparison to female English speakers who "often sound harsh, raucous, rude or overly masculine to a Japanese ear" (1967: 8). Emphatically male phonological markers include an 'r' trill and sound changes in certain adjectival endings[28] while nasality, little lip movementt and raised volume characterize males on the phonetic level.

As for grammatical gender markers, it has already been mentioned that women employ honorifics to a greater extent than males (cf. Peng et al. 1981). They tend to restrict the non-honorific, plain style to immediate family members, close friends and children but use honorifics to their husbands. Generally, women tend to be one level politer than men: "a polite form that would be used by a man only when talking to a person of extremely high position might be used by a woman in talking to a casual acquaintance." (Jorden 1983: 251) Thus, males tend to use plain imperatives for making requests, e.g. *koi* ('come here') and *ikō* ('let's go), while females would make such a request or suggestion with a referent honorific, e.g. *irrashai* ('come here') or an addressee honorific *ikimashō* ('let's go').

There are also certain sentence final particles which are particularly associated with a speaker's sexual identity[29]. The semantic function of female-associated particles involves both the softening and emphasizing of utterance content while male ones suggest greater assertiveness and virility[30]. Although the forms themselves are neither feminine nor masculine as such, it is their frequent employment by one sex in particular situations that has led to their association with gender.

However, these particles as with other gender-related markers mentioned in this section are not employed in all situations but their occurrence depends on participants[31] and definitions of the setting and topic. In most transactional (non-private) encounters, sexually neutral language[32] is usually evident: "A young woman may use feminine language in talking to her mother about a new kimono, but a sexually neutral or masculine style in discussing history in the college classroom ... The Japanese grand-mother who uses feminine speech in her conversations with women friends, often switches to brusque, rather masculine speech in the home, reflecting her social position". (Jorden 1983: 251) Moreover, among younger males there has been a distinct move to a politer style that is considered as 'feminine' by the conservatively-minded. It should also be noted that Japanese males also use forms associated with females when expressing empathy or gentleness and particularly when talking to children or the infirm[33].

On a lexical level, the use of certain first person pronouns such as *atashi*, *atakushi* are reserved for females while *boku* and the more aggressive *ore* are only used by males for self-reference. Then there are second person pronouns which also relate to speaker sex, e.g. women use *kimi* (you) only with intimates or those of inferior status, but men may employ it for strangers and in any situation. Certain 'rougher' second person pronouns are restricted for men such as *omae* and *kisama*. As for third person pronouns, Hinds (1975) finds that females use *kare* (he) more than males but never to family members or social superiors since it carries special emotional connotations if employed by women.

Another area of lexical selection has to do with the avoidance of Chinese loans that are too 'complicated' for females. Ide (1982) also mentions the case of "beautification honorifics" as another marker of female style; these are "different from referent and addressee honorifics in that they are used only to beautify speech" and are not verb forms but involve, for example, the extensive attachment of the (respect-marking) prefix *o-* to everyday nouns, sometimes even leading to hypercorrection.

As stated above, the variable of sex has not been shown to be significant in the employment of standard versus dialect varieties but further substantiation of this is necessary in the light of world research which indicates that women may conform more to the standard than men (cf. Smith 1979: 120-1).

Another dimension of gender-related language behaviour has to do with the distribution of speaking rights. Japanese females are generally expected in formal situations to talk much less than males or even remain silent; In the study of a wedding reception described in chapter 2 in this volume it can be seen how the bride and all other leading female participants are denied the opportunity to speak and how seven out of the eight wedding speeches are given by men with only one, final speech given by a woman. Even though males are assigned greater speaking rights than women, the masculine ideal is a low linguistic profile of terse, self-restrained verbal communication which is accompanied by stern faces and stiff postures.

Finally, the phenomenon of linguistic sex deviancy in Japan also deserves consideration. Pharr (1976: 38), for instance, observes how female activists in the Japanese Red Army "spoke with great frankness and directness. In many cases they used plain forms of speech (i.e. no honorifics) and numerous expressions that are commonly regarded as men's language". Furthermore, *kabuki* female impersonators frequently adopt women's language when off stage in public (media) interaction; this seems totally acceptable to the Japanese speech community. At first sight, this seems to contradict the claim that there is social pressure to rigidly conform in sexually-specific behaviour but is in fact connected to expectations of (cross-sexual) role enactment.

Other areas which need fuller investigation are male/female differences in paralanguage (degree of laughter), kinesics (kneeling, eye and mouth movement) and rhetoric patterns (strategies of ambiguity and directness).

1.3.2.2. *Age markers*

Only a few dynamic markers of age[34] will be considered here. As Helfrich (1979: 64) states, the invariant correlation of linguistic markers with age is rare and the relationship is usually one of probability.

It has already been pointed out above that age is a significant variable in the employment of dialect and standard varieties. Nomoto's (1975) discussion of data on the standardization process collected in 1971, shows how the younger the informants, the greater is their conformity to the standard: the 15-19 age group produce 96.5% standard responses with respect to phonetic quality while the 55-69 age group produce only 62.9%. Whether this situation remains stable, i.e. whether the young group maintain their present level of standard performance, is not certain, particularly since other research (quoted in Grootaers 1982) indicates that a reversion to dialect occurs after 20, when as young adults they assume responsibilities in the local community. However, it is not suggested here that dialect itself is a marker of age but that its employment with non in-group interlocutors tends to correlate with middle-aged speakers and the elderly.

A further possible marker of age is the ability to use recent English loans which are a favourite of youth and pop culture, mass media and fashion trends (cf. 1.5.1.). Thus, Ishino (1983) discovered that for certain borrowings there can be a 63% gap on acceptability as Japanese, depending on the age of informants[35].

The pronunciation of earlier established German loans and newer related English loans e.g. *zemināru/ seminā* (seminar) are another potential age differentiating variable as is also phonological innovation involving the expansion of vowel devoicing[36] which is spreading among urban youth and seriously affecting the acoustic perception of the CVCV structure of the language.

On the grammatical level, there is a general correlation between the degree of honorific usage and age: middle-aged and elderly speakers employing them to a greater extent in more situations. Furthermore, competence in reference honorifics seems more difficult for younger speakers (cf. Inoue 1979).

Helfrich's (1979) distinction between "sender age markers" and "receiver age markers"[37] is also important here in that it is a ground rule of Japanese sociolinguistic behaviour to be polite to older persons (cf. Ide 1982: 368-371), particularly due to the historical influence of Confucianism. The seniority system operating within all Japanese social groups is based on age as the rank-defining criterion. On the other hand, social position and power are more important values than age so that a person will be polite, for example, to a doctor that is younger in age. Moreover, "reciprocity is observed when rules come into conflict. A customer will be polite to a salesperson, as a teacher will be to a student's parent. Likewise, in those situations where age plays a role, a younger doctor will be reciprocally polite to an older person, as a younger superior will be to an older but subordinate person" (Ide 1982: 369).

Lastly, in this section Japanese baby-talk will be mentioned as a case of receiver age-markers and on which (to my knowledge) no research is available. Widely reported cross-cultural characteristics of baby-talk such as reduplication, phonological reduction and special voice quality such as high pitch and labialization can all be found in Japan where baby-talk is used well beyond babyhood into kindergarten and even early schooling. Special features include the frequent use of the female-associated, final particles *yo* and *ne*[29], the beautification honorific prefix exceptionally used for referring to one's own possessions, e.g. *o-uchi* (home), *o-tete* (hands), and the omission of grammatical particles (which mark the subject and object of an utterance) which is part of a structural simplification.

Sociolinguistically more interesting are the cases when the receivers of baby-talk are adults. This 'affected' speech style seems widespread among teenage girls and those in their early twenties. It inversely symbolizes child-like innocence and calls for the protection of the speaker, tending to occur where the receiver is seen as adopting a caretaker role. This adult-to-adult form of baby-talk emphasizes the perceived passivity and dependence of its producer. In this connection it is worth considering the Japanese concept of *amae* which basically refers to "the feelings that all normal infants at the breast harbor toward the mother — dependence, the desire to be passively loved, and the unwillingness to be separated from the warm mother-child circle and cast into a word of objective 'reality' (Doi 1973: 7), a feeling which is prolonged and diffused through adulthood in Japan so that adults deliberately act in a way to seek others' indulgence; it is reflected in various forms of sociolinguistic behaviour (cf. Doi 1977).

1.3.2.3. *Group identity markers*

Lebra (1976) has claimed that it is primarily on the basis of group ties that Japanese establish identities. The ordinary workings of the Japanese language make it impossible to converse without clearly indicating to which group the interlocutors or the persons they are talking about belong. This group identity is inferrable from interaction through, for example, the employment of honorifics, donatory verbs (cf. chapter 3), terms of address and reference as well as socially more indexical signs such as dialect, slang and other special (professional) registers.

The Japanese social nexus is, from a Western perspective, extremely limited which means that the linguistic homogeneity of the group is very high[38]. According to Nakane (1974), who sees Japan as a vertically structured society whose members are bound in tightly organized groups, such affiliations will only include the family, co-villagers of one's household and co-workers in the same section or division or the same factory building. This strong sense of inward versus external connections (*uchi to soto*) fosters a deep sense of solidarity and corporate identification.

In Japan it would seem that the only case of *major* group marking is that of dialect which serves as a marker of regional group identity. The markers of age and gender discussed above can and do serve as group markers since males and females are not encouraged (permitted to) mix socially as much as in the West after childhood, with the prevalence of monosexual groupings which are age-graded at school (even in co-eds), at university and at work.

One of the most discussed areas in the West with regard to sociolinguistic group identities is social class membership. According to a poll conducted in 1985[39], 88.5% of those Japanese surveyed said they regarded themselves as middle class, with only 0.5% identifying themselves as upper class and 8.1%

as lower class. This again reveals the strong sense of homogeneity in this nation. Little work in how class and language relate in Japan has been undertaken but honorific competence and reciprocal use of addressee honorifics seem to function as indicators of higher class membership.

The Japanese aristocracy was abolished at the end of World War II and it was known to heavily employ superpolite honorific forms within the family. The imperial family today still maintains a distinctly different vocabulary from the rest of the Japanese for certain items of food, furnishing, clothing and 'embarrassing' matters connected with money and death as well as special terms for addressing kin which is due to the conservation of medieval court usage (cf. Sakurai 1984). Nominal honorification e.g. *o-moji* 'obi sash', *o-mō-sama* 'father', onomatopoetic reduplication e.g. *zoro-zoro* 'fine somen noodles' (based on the sound of sucking noodles into the mouth), different character readings from common use and re-naming items on the basis of their shape, colour or composition are some of the devices this court language employs.

The command of lexical repertoire may also serve as a potential indication of group membership (cf. Brown and Levinson 1979: 309-312) and Japanese society provides many such cases. For example, the restricted register of the underworld[40] "which is specifically designed to (be) ... unintelligible to nonmembers of the group" (Brown and Levinson 1979: 310) involves syllabic reduction e.g. *satsu < keisatsu* 'police', syllabic exchange e.g. *su-gara < gara-su* 'glass', pronunciation change based on the multiple pronunciations available for a character e.g. *ken-ji-ru* instead *mi-ru* 'to see', borrowing from archaic, dialectal or foreign innovations e.g. *pēpā* (lit. 'paper') = 'forged notes' and lexical substitution e.g. *kodomo* (lit. 'child') = saké (cf. Lewin 1981: 1773-1774).

Other ingroup argots include those of soldiers, seamen, adolescents, the political underground, beggars and students. The linguistic behaviour of the last of these groups has a strong influence on everyday language and many of their innovations eventually find their way into the standard variety. Student in-group language (*gakusei-go*) is characterized by
– its strong tendency to borrow foreign loans accompanied often by word play, e.g. *macdonaru* (> McDonald's) 'to badger with questions'; *adaruto* (> adult) *suru* 'to dress formally and conservatively'; *charinko* (> Korean 'bicycle') = 'stealing'; metaphoric use of loans, e.g. *supagetti* = 'mixed up'; forming new words by borrowed suffixes e.g. *ojin-chikku* (> ojin + tic) = 'old', *kae-ringu* (> kaeru + ing) 'going home';

– borrowing from hoodlum jargon e.g. *dachiko* 'buddy'; *baso* 'buckwheat noodles'

– lexical creativity e.g. *chikuru* 'to tell tales' (> *tsugeguchi suru*); *bai-nara* (bye + *sayonara*); adding verbs to nouns, e.g. *cha-suru* 'drinking coffee in a coffee shop', *nanpa-suru* 'girl hunting';

– syllabic clipping e.g. *ippan-kyōiku* 'general education course' > *pan-kyo*; *kissaten* 'coffee shop' > *saten*;

– phonetic features such as stressing or lengthening of last vowels in utterances, heavy stress on particles and rising intonation at the end of clauses as well as omission of particles.

This restless pursuit of linguistic novelty is an indication of the general linguistic fancifullness which the Japanese enjoy while at the same time it reflects the fact that university students can afford to play around with language, desiring to mark themselves off from the mainstream by their no-conformist in-talk.

Certain occupational jargons were studied as far back as 50 years ago such as the historical styles of monks and prostitutes (cf. Kikuzawa 1936).

The symbolization of group identity is a field which yields many significant insights into the culture-specific dynamics of Japan and clearly deserves more attention from researchers in the future.

1.4. Language attitudes

First of all, certain cultural beliefs concerning the Japanese language which are part of a folk linguistic inheritance that also enter into Japanese academic linguistics will be considered. These folk notions serve to support and strengthen the speech-community and promote the traditional linguistic monolithism of Japan.

In contrast to present-day Western linguistics which does not participate in the scientific support of prescriptivism or other types of prejudice-based ideology, Japanese scholars[41] have been accused of actively propagating and sustaining ethnocentric notions that proclaim the uniqueness and superiority of the Japanese language, its inexpressability, untranslatibility and unlearnability by non-Japanese as well as its extraordinary spiritual power[42] (cf. Miller 1977 and 1982).

An apparent contradiction of this folk ideology is the belief in the inadequacies of Japanese which is expressed in statements such as Japanese is imperfect, impractical, lacking in 'proper' grammar or lexical resources, or in need of replacement. Miller (1982: 125) views this negativeness merely as the other side of the same coin: "The essence of the modern myth of Nihongo is that the language is worthy of honour and love and respect, but ... Always present and immediately available on an adjacent, intimately accessible dimension is the direct opposite: love is countered by hate, pleasure by pain, affection and concern by Schadenfreude".

Moreover, Miller claims that the Japanese experience a negative reaction to the spectacle of non-Japanese employing the language with any degree of fluency: "A foreigner speaking Japanese amounts to the public performance of an unnatural act" (1977: 84) due to an absolutist identification of ethnicity with language. However, this only applies to Caucasians; Koreans, Chinese, Southeast Asians and even Indians are expected to know Japanese if they live or work in Japan for extended periods "and it is surely no accident that for several decades following World War II the only Japanese language training program provided for non-Japanese by the government was a small language school that specialized exclusively in teaching the language to Southeast Asians and other nonwhites" (1977: 78).

An interesting reflection of attitudes towards non-Japanese including Caucasians is shown in the representation of their L1 speech, i.e. when they are speaking their own native language — as it is dubbed on sound tracks or written in modern Japanese publications: "This is perfectly intelligible and fluent Japanese, but would never for a moment be mistaken for the Japanese spoken by Japanese, from which system it is separated by a significant bundling of isoglosses" (Miller 1971: 622-3). Miller identifies features such as differing word order with address terms coming at the end of sentences or the use of katakana syllabic orthography. From my own observations, I would add odd turns of phrase that are literal translations from Western languages and a recognizably different voice quality. However, it is not marked as reduced or simplified unless the non-Japanese are encoding their message in Japanese when it almost invariably is. It does not seem to be related to the portrayal of lower status (cf. Valdman 1981) so much as the embodiment of the myth of unlearnability.

On the other hand, it is important to temper Miller's claims with a study conducted by Saint-Jacques (1983) which refutes the notion that Japanese should only be spoken by ethnic Japanese. The findings of this survey show that most of the Japanese interviewed (who had experience of Japanese-speaking non-Japanese) were overwhelmingly in favour of being addressed in Japanese by foreigners (94%) and liked to speak Japanese to foreigners (96%) while 97% of the interviewed Japanese-speaking foreign residents of

Tokyo stated that the Japanese answered them in Japanese, enjoyed communicating with them in Japanese and did not find that their knowledge of the language created suspicion or mistrust but only aided and fostered interaction.

A further attitude that has received little attention is the conception that the current extent of Western borrowings is leading to language 'decline' or 'infection' and is a sign that the Japanese have lost faith in their own linguistic creativity — and beyond this, their own culture as represented by language in the process of modernization.

Many other Japanese attitudes require full investigation: the heavy respect given to the written language over speech[43], language-related superstitions such as talismen (*mamori*) bearing a character, chants and incantations, naming practices based on astrology, taboo terms for discriminated groups and professions[44] and attitudes towards minority languages[45].

Finally, in this section Japanese attitudes towards speech as revealed in a study of native proverbs by Fischer and Yoshida (1968) will be discussed. There are a wealth of sayings which extol the virtues of silence[46], warn against the dangers of gossip and free-speech, advocate consultation and exalt the value of a small commitee which, in a sense, minimizes the individual's abilities to solve problems alone. Suspiciousness about speech and the need to speak carefully also emerge as important notions resulting from the importance of restrained behaviour in fixed social networks[47].

1.4.1. *Language planning*

Folk attitudes to language may and often do find official recognition, coming to constitute politically organized language planning[48] which has been carried out in Japan since the beginning of this century[49]. The gradual emergence of present-day standard Japanese was the result of various efforts and developments started in the Meiji era (from 1868 onwards) which were directed at (i) overcoming the prevailing diglossic situation (cf. 3.1.2.), (ii) finding a style suitable as a vehicle for modern Western conceptual systems, e.g. science, law, economics, politics and philosophy, (iii) dealing with the lack of a single, national variety for written or oral communication.

According to Neustupny (1983), the standardization of Japanese was a relatively uncontrolled process in its early phases (1868-1900) and was neither directly related to individual innovations[50] nor linguistic pressure groups such as the movement for 'the unification of speech and writing'[51] and the societies calling for the romanized transcription of Japanese[52] who were not taken as seriously as the campaigners for the abandonment of Chinese characters and the sole employment of the syllabaries[53].

By the beginning of this century, a literary-spoken style had crystalized principally in fiction which ignored the fossilized, feudalistic inheritance of a heavily Sinicized superstructure and oriented itself to the progressive and prestigious, urban variety of the new capital, Tokyo[54].

However, although a considerable amount of fictional literature and educational texts were produced using this newly constructed 'literary-spoken language' (kōgo-tai) and the press of the Taisho period (1915-1926) partially adopted it, the government and its agencies maintained the High Sinicized written variety until American Occupation authorities forced reforms after the war[55] (cf. Müller 1975).

Westernization and modernization, of course, led to the need for massive borrowing and this area underwent some official control in the 1930's[56], when standardizing lexica appeared, although no rigorous language planning ever took place. The war brought a banning and replacement of English loans in the media and daily usage (where possible). English education ceased at most schools and universities. Today, government publications still scrupulously avoid direct loans as much as possible.

Increased accessibility to the written language, resulting in the current official estimate of 99% literacy[57], has been facilitated by mass education and government reforms reducing the number of characters for daily use. In 1873, Fukuzawa Yukichi, founder of Keio University, proposed the ultimate abolition of Chinese characters and, as the first step, their reduction to two or three thousand. The major language planning activity of the Education Ministry has been connected with this question for which it has established various bodies[56]. Official orthograpic reform[58] seriously began at the end of the Second World War with two Cabinet decrees of 1946 limiting the characters for everyday use (tōyō kanji) to 1,850[59] and simplifying the syllabaries on a more phonetic basis. Two years later in 1948, the varying pronunciations of the characters were fixed and the characters to be taught in the first six school years laid down. In 1949 the diverging written forms for characters were restricted; in 1951 a special list of 92 characters for the use of personal names was issued and in 1959 the Cabinet produced rules for the syllabic spelling accompanying characters. These innovatory reforms were originally believed to be only the first, democraticizing steps towards a more radical simplification, unification and standardization of Japanese orthography — including the ultimate abandonment of the characters — as desired by American educational advisers of the Occupation Authorities[55]. However, no subsequent liberalizing reforms ever materialized.

Neustupný (1983: 31) maintains that since the 1960's language planning activity has been "distinctily anti-reformist" as the National Language Council (*Kokugo-shingikai*) has promulgated various measures to weaken earlier restrictions imposed on the public: the number of characters for basic school education was raised from 881 to 996 in 1968, the number of approved readings for daily characters increased in 1973 and the list of approved daily characters extended to 1,945 in 1981. "The new language treatment measures seem to command the support not merely of the Old Right, which interprets them as a sign of commencing revival, but of the public in general ... There is also no doubt that they take no regard of the language problems of those classes of the Japanese society which do not possess the advantage of higher education" (Neustupný 1983: 30). Clearly, a liberalization of Japanese orthographic practices is not foreseeable in the decades ahead.

Finally, the governmental promotion of Japanese as a second language will be considered as this is also part of language planning. During Japan's colonization of Korea (1910-1945) and Taiwan (1895-1945) Japanese was the obligatory, official medium in administrative and educational domains; the study of Korean language and culture was banned from the school curriculum.

Although the Pekingese variety of Mandarin Chinese was the official language of the Manchurian state of Manchukuo, under Japanese control (1934-1945), Japanese was a mandatory school subject as in all Japanese occupied territories of S.E. Asia where, interestingly enough, certain local languages and forms of local nationalism were promoted while English suppressed, e.g. in Singapore and Malaysia, Japanese and Malay were declared official languages with Tamil also taught in schools but Mandarin and English were removed (Platt and Weber 1980: 36); in the Philippines, the Japanese Military Administration proved very effective in advancing the cause of Tagalog which became for the first time an official language together with Japanese, and government officials and employees were told not to use English (Asuncion-Landé and Pascasio 1979: 215).

These developments were connected to an extensive, nationalistic second language policy[60] under the direction of the Society for the Promotion of Japanese Language Education (*Nihon Bunka Kyōkai*), established in 1940, and a similar organization, the Association for the Advancement of Japanese (*Nihon-Kyōiku-Shinkō-kai*), attached to the Ministry of Culture and the

Ministry of Greater East Asian Affairs in 1941.

In 1972 a government agency called the Japanese Foundation (*Kokusai-kōryū-kikin*) was set up which actively organizes the teaching of Japanese to non-natives and runs various research support programmes. The spread and promotion of the Japanese language are its aims. The current head of the Japanese Studies Department of the Japan Foundation, Shiina Kazuo, recently stated[61]: "It is my desire that the Japanese language be given another look as a means of communication in internationalized modern society" and Nomoto Kikuo, director-general of the National Japanese Language Research Institute, another government organization, declared[61]: "Inasmuch as spreading of the Japanese language would also result in an increased number of pro-Japanese, it is worth spending more money on the diffusion of the language and this is important". There is a widely voiced satisfaction, at the political and pedagogical level, with the growing number of foreigners currently engaged in the acquisition of Japanese: about 190,000[62] in the mid 1980's. Earnest discussion concerning how to officially encourage more foreign students to study in Japan is now underway with hopes of 100,000 by the early 21st century[62].

1.5. Contact between Japanese and other languages in sociolinguistic perspective

As employed here, the term 'language contact' refers to an extremely broad range of phenomena which relate to the direct or indirect influences of foreign languages on Japanese. These influences have occurred on every linguistic level, although not necessarily for each language contact. Nearly all research has focussed on the structural aspects of Japanese language contacts but there are many sociolinguistically significant dimensions that should be considered which throw light on Japanese foreign relations and internal cultural development. Due to space limitations, only a brief review of the topic is offered below.

The most intense contact of Japanese with another language has been the case of Chinese, going back to the end of the 4th century A.D. when the Japanese, with no means of writing of their own, adopted Chinese characters wholesale — and the contemporary variety of Chinese with them. Initially the Chinese language was employed for official records and religious texts until historical events[63] and linguistic developments led to the official use of a heavily Sinicized Japanese in the Heian period. Particularly the consolidation of the syllabaries, which became widely known by the 10th century, allowed for a more accurate representation of Japanese since the Chinese characters had been constructed for an analytic language unlike Japanese. From the Heian period onwards, extensive borrowing from Chinese occurred and mixed, Sino-Japanese writing styles also emerged, both effects of the long period of (written) diglossic bilingualism. In fact, until the beginning of this century, formal written varieties were so modelled that their surface appearance could pass for Chinese. The number of Chinese loans (47.5%) exceeds that of native Japanese words: 36.7% (Japanese National Language Research Institute, 1964). The Chinese impetus for the development of early Japanese civilization was crucial and sociocultural-linguistic contacts vigorously renewed during a second Chinese wave from the 15th century to mid-19th century. The Chinese heritage is vast and still strongly evident.

In sharp contrast to the Chinese permeation of the Japanese world, the influence of other Asian languages on Japanese is negligible. This, of course, reflects the attitude and relations of the Japanese towards these other communities. Ainu[64], for example, an indigenous language to Japan and now on the verge of extinction, has been in contact with Japanese since the 8th century but is only discernible in a few place names and a handful of loans related to the ecological sphere, e.g. salmon (*sake*), seaweed (*kombu*). The Ainu were historically considered enemies[65] and are still held to be less sophisticated than the Japanese whose culture advanced beyond that of the Ainu under early Sinicization. Inspite of geographical proximity, social distance has prevented interaction and borrowing. The situation is comparable somewhat to the limited linguistic contact between English and the indigenous languages of Australia and New Zealand.

Koreans played a formative role in the cultural and political growth of early Japan and are supposed to have been responsible for the adaptation of Chinese characters to the Japanese language which later led to the syllabaries, yet surprisingly, very little linguistic contact has been uncovered. Most of the few Korean loans, which have only recenty been identified, entered Japanese before the 8th century[66]. Contacts were renewed after Japan's colonization of Korea in 1910 but the sociocultural dominance was reversed. A few Koreanisms of a stylistically non-standard character have entered modern Japanese[67], introduced by Japanese repatriates returning from Korea as well as possibly the Korean immigrant community in Japan.

Contact with European languages began as far back as the 16th century when Portuguese and Spanish traders and missionaries came to Japan. Today 200 words from these languages are still employed particularly for daily items

of food and clothing[68]. When Japan closed its doors to these potential coloniz-
ers, it decided to maintain limited contact with the purely commercial Dutch
and so from 1640 until 1854 Dutch was Japan's sole medium of gaining access
to Western knowledge. The study of the language was practised as a secret,
hereditary art carried out by a few officially authorized interpreter families.
Borrowing and calques of terminology in fields such as medicine, astronomy,
botany, physics and military technology were particularly numerous and
many such loans are still in use[69]. In fact, Dutch remained the language of dip-
lomacy for dealing with the Western powers right up until 1870 when it was
replaced by English. Furthermore, it should be noted that until the end of the
Second World War the position of German rivalled that of English in certain
areas, the former being widely taught at universities and used in medical
study and diagnosis. There was considerable borrowing from German in
fields such as skiing, hiking, academics, politics, philosophy, technology and
student slang.

A recent sociolinguistic study by Haarman (1984) shows how stereotype
conceptions and social values attached to foreign languages are expressed in
contemporary Japanese mass media and certain texts of which constitute a
form of "impersonal bilingualism" which has no equivalent in the monolingual interaction of everyday community life.

1.5.1. *The expansion of Anglo-Japanese*[70]

Borrowings from foreign languages other than Chinese are today all
clearly marked as non-Japanese due to their representation in the angular syl-
labary. In its intensive 19th century phase of Westernization and early modernization, the Japanese preferred calquing but today wholesale borrowing is
proceeding at what for many constitutes a too rapid rate[71], as the plethora of
loan-word dictionaries attest. One of these[72] lists 7,000 foreignisms in current
speech with more than half deriving from English. In a recent survey of Western loans in the press, Morito (1978) discovered 94% of them to be of English
origin which clearly demonstrates the central position of English as the principal contact language of Japanese today. Stanlaw (1982) estimates that 8%
of the contemporary Japanese lexicon is English-based, but, of course, this
figure takes no account of the frequency of occurrence of English-derived
lexemes.

The current adoption and integration of English into Japanese is so
extensive that Passin (1980) sees it as significant as the massive borrowing
from Chinese in the Heian period. This English contact does not merely

involve the filling of linguistic gaps and meeting the needs of an industrial and post-industrial society but also involves the following:

- RE-LEXIFICATION, e.g. many abstract English-derived loans (assimilated to Japanese phonology) have Japanese equivalents, e.g. young, money, wife, happy, soft, rice, house; English terms have infiltrated and replaced certain indigenous taxonomies so that 52% of flower names, 30% of fruit, 35% of vegetables and 24% of animal designation is English-derived[73];
- LANGUAGE CHANGE such as loss of inflectional productivity and traditional numeral classifiers[74];
- various forms of NATIVIZATION[75] such as
  *semantic change of originally transferred items, e.g. (i) restriction: 'milk' only refers to the condensed kind; (ii) shift: 'cunning' refers to 'cheating in exams'; (iii) extension: 'dry' means 'business-like';
  *pseudo-English innovation, e.g. *skinship* (= physical closeness), *nighter* (= a baseball game played at night), *base-up* (= raise in basic salary);
  *truncated compounds, e.g. *han-suto* > 'hunger strike', *wā-pro* > 'word processor', *en-suto* > 'engine stop';
  *acronaming, e.g. OL (office lady), LDK (living-dining-kitchen), NHK (Nippon-hōsō-kyōkai), JNR (Japan National Railway);
  *hybridization, e.g. *dai-sutoraiku* > Jap. 'big' + Eng. 'strike', *terebi-kko* > Eng. 'television' + Jap. 'child';
- stylistic experimentation that comes close to CODE-MIXING[76], especially in advertising language, e.g. *Dynamic* na *design* de *tropical mood* afureru *leisure wear* ya ... *sharp* na *point* o tsukeru *accessory* o ...[77]

Most studies of this phenomenon have limited their focus to the structural adoption of English into Japanese[78]. An exception is Higa's (1979) simplistic explanation of the contact situation as one of subordination to a dominant, advanced society, America, and the naive conception of the number of borrowings as a relative index of Japanese cultural growth. Stanlaw (1982) is the only serious sociolinguistic attempt so far to grapple with this multifaceted problem, briefly touching on aspects such as the attitudes towards loans and their use by university students[79].

However, the sociocultural motivation for this contact is highly complex and must also relate to the symbolic value of English as a world lingua franca, its international employment for scientific, academic and commercial purposes, Japanese growing bilingualism in English, internal social desires concerning image and levels of sophistication that seem to be satisfied through an appeal to English linguistic resources and the exploitation of these feelings by advertising and mass media, both of which play a decisive and innovative role in Japanese society. The principal source of contact today does seem to be American varieties transmitted orally (via video, film, cassette, record as well as a limited degree of face-to-face interaction) and in written form through all types of publications. The main Japanese agents of dissemination are copy-writers, journalists, media personnel, translators and academics.

The function of loans is inextricably tied up to their contexts of occurrence. In some cases, they are purely decorative as when printed on clothing and bags, food and other made-in-Japan products[80] while in other cases they may serve stylistic purposes, e.g. provide euphemisms particularly for the sex industry or constitute lexical resources for the underworld[81] or fuse into a playful bilingual style in popular songs and media. Above all, Anglo-Japanese seems to symbolize modernity, rather than modernization, and expresses the Japanese acquisition of Westerness.

In a way, the phenomenon contradicts the traditional view of the Japanese as 'insular' and shows their sense of sociolinguistic prestige to be stronger than their conservatism and ethnocentrism. If the present developments are permitted to continue, a high level of societal bilingualism in English will be necessary by the end of the century. However, now in the mid-80's there is a widely noted failure of English L2 education which has concentrated exclusively on university entrance tests which require the ability to translate written English into Japanese.

1.5.2. *Japanese-based pidgins*[82]

So far a number of Japanese-related pidgins have been reported but they are now nearly all only historical cases. These pidgins seem to fulfill the 'classic' criteria of limited function and restricted social contact of interactants unfamiliar with each others' languages.

1. A 19th century pidgin[83] developed for trading situations between Westerners and Japanese particularly in Yokohama but also Kobe and Nagasaki (cf. Daniels 1948). 85% of its vocabulary derived from Japanese but it included words from various English varieties (Chinese and Indian) as well as Malay and French items. It is supposed to have acted as a transmitting agent of early English loans into Japanese. Structurally, it is said to have been strongly influenced by Japanese.

2. During the Second World War various pidgins were developed in areas occupied by the Japanese forces, some were still in use immediately after the

war as in Singapore between Malays and Western army personnel[84]. The presence of the American Occupation Forces after the war in Japan also led to the emergence of a pidgin which Norman (1954) calls "Japanese Bamboo English", employed by Japanese with limited English knowledge in commercial and working contact with American GI's (cf. Goodman 1967). It seems to have involved American 'foreigner talk' and been structurally and phonologically more English-influenced but with many Japanese local terms. Algeo (1966) discussses how it was maintained during the Korean War and extended to include Korean vocabulary.

3. The fullest described Japanese pidgin (cf. Nagara 1972 and Reinecke 1969), is that of the Japanese immigrant laborers to Hawaii from 1885 onwards. It is only this first generation which used Japanese Pidgin English which was closely related to Plantation Pidgin English, a lingua franca spoken by Hawaiian and Chinese co-workers and English and Portuguese supervisors at the time. The Japanese pidgin was not maintained by the second generation who shifted to Hawaiian Creole English now in various stages of decreolization (cf. Nagata 1984) and standard English as the Japanese community became increasingly urban and upwardly mobile.

1.5.3. *Japanese overseas communities*

Information on the Japanese immigrant communities in South America is sparse[86]. The largest concentration is in Brazil (491,000) with emigration started in 1908 and where a language shift in favour of Portuguese as L1 is particularly evident among the third generation and in urban areas. Lack of Japanese education, a semi-bilingual second generation fully proficient in neither Brazilian nor Portuguese and strong integrative motivation are the likely causes. The Japanese employed tends to be archaic (acquired from elderly family members) and replaces the English loans of mainland Japanese with Portuguese equivalents e.g. *chokorēto* > *shokorāte*. Japanese is, however maintained in the domains of ethnic media (newspapers) and religious practice. There are also Japanese communities in Peru (45,000) and Argentina.

As for the contemporary Japanese community in Hawaii which constitutes one quarter (240,000) of the entire population of the islands, it is often noted that the third generation have shifted entirely to English and no longer have command of their ethnic tongue. However, post-war immigrants from Japan have helped to maintain Japanese for certain media. During the Second World War the community discouraged the use of Japanese among its members which aided its decline. Higa's (1975) study of the extensive English borrowing in contemporary Hawaiian Japanese shows how it creates a special identity and sense of solidarity for its speakers. Japanese has influenced Hawaiian English lexically and structurally (cf. Glissmeyer 1973). Ogawa (1979) discusses authoritarian "familial values" and their effect on communication in Japanese families in Honolulu resulting in greater silence and less answering back than in other ethnic groups.

The number of Japanese descendants living in the USA numbers 465,000 as of 1980[87]. Waggoner (1981) estimates the US population with Japanese as mother tongue to be 405,000 but only 95,000 of these claim to use Japanese in the home. This last figure shows the lack of interest in maintaining Japanese in the younger generations, which is a reflection of a stigmatized past stemming from strong anti-Japanese sentiment during and following World War II and the forced re-settlement of all ethnic Japanese (even those with American citizenship) in camps for the duration. Suzuki (1976) offers a description of the language contact in these 'relocation camps', mentioning aspects such as code-switching, distinct differences between generations in use of English and a complex concerning the non-native character of Japanese-influenced English. Today, Japanese Americans are the most successful non-white group to assimilate into maintream society and many have disassociated themselves from their Japanese identity. For example, Beltramo (1981: 376) describes the recent case of a local Japanese group in Montana who declined to participate in a meeting on local ethnic heritage with the statement that they no longer considered themselves as a distinct ethnic group. Some research on Japanese American bilinguals has been conducted by Ervin-Tripp (1968) who shows how asking the same question in either of the languages evokes different value-related responses.

Finally, the temporary Japanese communities of businessmen, diplomats, correspondents and advisers and their families require consideration. Bolitho (1976) presents a rare analysis of such a group, focussing on the communicative networks of Japanese women temporarily resident in Melbourne and how the latter form links with members of the Australian community. It appears that various types of either ethnically or non-ethnically oriented networks exist which relate to many social factors. Another related area is the situation of the 'returning youngsters' (*Nihonjin-kikoku-shijo*) who encounter educational and social difficulties[89] on termination of their period abroad which has led often to a bilingual and bicultural condition. At present, 51,000 Japanese of school-age undergo schooling overseas. Various aspects are involved here such as code-switching, language shift and language attrition among others. Okamura-Bichard (1985) reports on a study of mother-tongue maintenance and L2 learning of Japanese children whose parents are temporarily resident in the USA which found that there were no relationships between the years of schooling in Japan and level of Japanese language skill but that the years of schooling in the US significantly related to English skill level. Parents proved an important factor in mother tongue maintenance but the children's own interests, attitudes and the extent of using either language contributed more significantly to the level in each language.

1.5.4. *Cross-cultural communication*

Finally, the topic of Japanese interacting with other peoples deserves attention, especially as economic growth is leading to increasing international contact. Loveday (1982b) examines the communicative problems of Japanese performing in English resulting from contrasts in sociocultural values attached to language use such as the Japanese underdifferentiation of talk reflected in greater silence, terseness and caution in speech, the lack of logical organization of discourse, the heavy emphasis on vertical politeness and depersonalising routine formulae[90], and the inability to communicate unless considerable social information concerning the interlocutor is available. Chapter 4, part 2, presents the problems that arise for Japanese and Westerners in trying to understand each other's verbal and non-verbal behaviour and the conflict which arises from their cross-cultural miscoding. There have been a few other studies in this field, cf. Barnlund's (1975) comparative investigation of self-revelation in Japan and America (see also Condon and Saito 1974).

1.6. Other topics in Japanese sociolinguistics

Not all areas of Japanese sociolinguistics have been discussed above. The main topic that has not been touched on is the anthropological concern with reflections of the kinship system in the Japanese language (cf. Befu and Norbeck 1958 and Prindle 1972) and Japanese folk classification systems, e.g. the many terms for rice[91]. Furthermore, pragmatic dimensions have not been treated; Japanese discourse has undergone intensive research by Hinds (1976a, 1976b, 1979, 1980, 1982a, 1982b and 1983) who has examined paragraph structure, turn signals, ellipsis, case marking in both Japanese written and oral texts, comparative rhetorics and typologized Japanese discourse. It appears that Japanese conversational interactants require less overt clues in the form of spoken words than do Westerners for successful communication supposedly because of the extreme homogeneity of the speech community.

Many sociolinguistic areas have hardly begun to be analyzed such as Japanese non-verbal behaviour (cf. Morsbach 1972), child language acquisition (cf. Fischer 1970 and Honna 1975), special cultural[92] texts and genres such as those of professional storytellers (*rakugo*) (cf. Hrdlickovà 1969 and Sanches 1975), and various naming practices, e.g. astrological consultation for naming newborns, naming ceremonies for sumo wrestlers and kabuki entertainers, nicknaming, naming in religion[93] and the highly symbolic value attached to names of peoples and objects[94].

1.7. Conclusion

The relation of the Japanese language to its sociocultural context is a vast and gradually growing field. The majority of research achievements have only been made since the 1970's and non-Japanese scholars have contributed considerably in introducing innovative approaches and significant insights. Although certain influential Japanese-language scholars have maintained their narrow, native paradigms which view Japanese as 'unique' and 'totally distinct' from all other speech-communities, those trained in foreign languages and Western linguistics are increasingly changing the style of research.

It is to be hoped that in the future indigenous Japanese sociolinguistics will completely break out of its academic ethnocentrism and more actively draw on information about outside communities for comparative purposes and aid in the construction of sociolinguistic universals as well as contribute more to international research. In Japanese sociolinguistics generally, there has unfortunately been an over-heavy emphasis on mere data-collection, and particularly its statistical aspects, so that greater theoretical elaboration and conceptual development constitute principal goals for the decades ahead.

2. THE ETHNOGRAPHY OF RITUAL AND ADDRESS AT A WEDDING RECEPTION

This chapter examines the linguistic organization of a Japanese wedding reception in order to understand the social construction of ritual and the dynamic, context-dependent meaning of address and reference. The analysis follows a Hymesian 'ethnography of speaking' approach (cf. Bauman and Sherzer 1974). Essential background information on Japanese concepts of family and marriage can be found in the Appendix on p.119 and consulting these notes may help the reader before starting the description of the reception below.

2.1. The reception: setting, participants, activities and functions

The wedding reception under discussion took place in Toki city, Gifu prefecture, on 4 October 1978. The reception was held in a large hall of a commercial organization offering a variety of services for weddings such as reception rooms, catering and costume-hire. Inside the hall were four rows of decorated tables arranged in a rectangle and laid out with trays of delicacies for each guest. At one end of the hall constituting the focal point of the event, is a golden screen in front of which sat the newly-weds, accompanied on each side by their ceremonial go-betweens or *baishakunin*[95].

The newly-weds' parents were seated at the opposite end of the hall directly facing their children at the front. The two fathers sat in the centre with their wives on either side. These spatial semiotics relate to notions of status and etiquette whereby guests are placed higher than the host. The groom's parents were a newly-established pottery producing family in Gifu and the bride's family came from Kyūshū, some 600 km away. The bride's father was a blue-collar worker employed by the prestigious Mitsubishi company. The hall had been symbolically divided into the groom's side and the bride's side, so that guests of the respective households sat apart at either of the two long tables between the front screen and parents' table.

Altogether there were 88 participants at the reception; there were five 'host' couples (the bride and groom, groom's parents, bride's parents and the two go-between couples for each newly-wed partner). There were altogether eight speech-givers, with six coming from the remaining 77 invited guests who were mainly composed of the groom's family's employees (11), business acquaintances (17), kindred (25), neighbours (5) and friends (6). The bride's fammily had only invited seven kin, three friends and three work-related guests (two of whom were speech-givers). As it is normal for only the couple's parents and a limited number of very close relatives and the go-betweens to attend the traditional Japanese wedding ceremony conducted by Shinto priests, the principal function of a wedding reception is to publicize and celebrate the union with the groom's kin and associates. The Japanese name for the event is *hirōen* which literally means an 'announcement banquet'[96]. The reception has a much wider social purpose than the actual marriage ceremony which only involves the contractual, nine-fold sipping of wine by the couple.

From discussions with participants and observation of the event, the principal functions of a contemporary Japanese wedding reception, apart from the obvious expression of family solidarity, appear to be:
– the promotion and proving of the credibility and acceptability of the newly-weds to their respective households, generally by implication of their parents' social standing, achievements, etc. which are mentioned in the speeches made;
– particularly the seeking of approbation from kindred, especially among the groom's relatives since marriage is viewed less as a union between a man and woman but more as the admittance of a woman to a husband's kin group[97];
– resulting from the above, the promotion of the newly-weds' social standing throughout the occasion by the presence of high status speakers and guests, by the entertaining of important business and professional acquaintances, here reflected in the seating arrangements, whereby such guests receive prominent front seats; and by the experiencing of pleasure, which is achieved through speeches, costume changes[98], singing and celebratory food.

The action of this reception was split into two sections: (i) the marriage announcement ceremony or *kekkon hirōshiki* which was significantly marked here by its traditional orientation with the couple wearing Japanese-style dress, and (ii) the congratulatory banquet or *hirōen no shukuen* which was Western-oriented, as reflected in the white wedding cake, candles, soft organ music and the change out of traditional dress into Western attire. Speeches constituted the sole activity of the first section — with the bride and groom standing throughout the announcement ceremony but sitting after the second speech given by the go-between representing the bride. After the fourth speech, a barrel of rice wine was opened by the couple and the banquet began, assuming an increasingly relaxed tone and culminating in the breaking of constraints by the groom's father's impromptu rendition of a folk song. Finally, the couple lit candles for each guest and then the groom's father and groom thanked guests who departed with a gift. It should be mentioned that apart from the couple, the go-betweens, parents and guests, there was also a master of ceremonies or *shikai* who introduced individual speech givers and organized the various movements rather like an orchestra conductor.

2.1.1. *The organization of speaking*

Altogether six speeches were given at the reception and Fig.2 shows how these speech givers related to the respective families of the groom and bride. From this figure it is clear that a balance between the various speech-givers was sought: four represented the groom and four represented the bride. It is also evident from the diagram that nearly all the selected speakers, who were related in some way to the two fathers (apart from the bride's go-between) came from the working spheres of the fathers[99]. What also emerged from the organization of the speeches was that the leading female participants i.e. the bride, the female go-betweens and the mothers had all been denied speaking rights. Similarly, the groom remained silent throughout the reception, only to say a few words of thanks after his father on its termination. In contrast, the bride's father never spoke nor sang.

Furthermore, the sequencing of the speeches reveals the dominant role of the groom's family throughout the event. It is interesting to note that the first Speech Giver (from now on referred to as SG1) was the groom's go-between. Another aspect worth noting is the hierarchy of ranking employed to distinguish the status of the individual speech givers in relation to each other e.g. the president of the pottery manufacturers' association (SG3 i.e. third speech giver) and SG4, the bride's father's former superior, were given the privelege of being placed nearer the beginning of the reception while the youngest speakers who directly represented the newly-weds (SG7 and SG8) were placed last in the order of speech-giving. The bride's representative was last because the bride holds lower status than the groom and his family's associates. Nevertheless, the fact that this last speaker was the only woman speech-giver should not be taken as overtly signifying that the status of a Japanese woman is automatically low. Were the bride's representative a man, he would also have spoken last, for status precedes sex in Japanese society. What is insightful here is that none of the speech-givers, apart from the

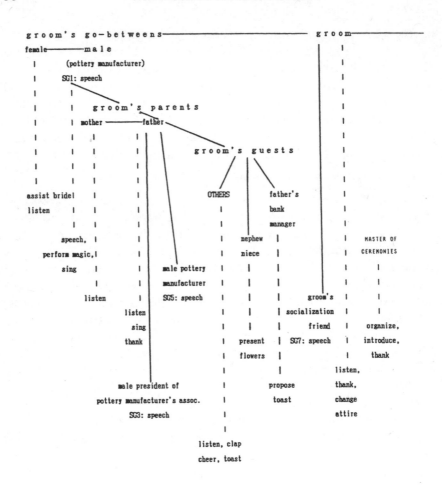

Fig. 2. The performance and relationships of participants at the wedding
         reception.
(The solid lines indicate the relationship between guests and households
while the dotted lines indicate acts performed. SG is an abbreviation for
*S*peech *G*iver and the number next to it relates to speech giving order.)

bride's representative were women — which suggests that females are
inferiors in this type of event because they have not attained the status necessary to be on a par with men. Such sequencing of the reception's turn-taking
system is obviously based on a hierarchic frame of reference.

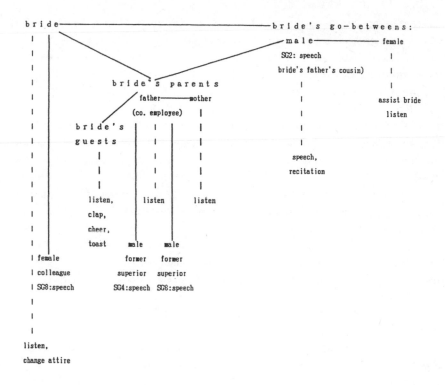

2.2. The linguistic components of ritual

The term ritual is open to various interpretations depending on the theories of ethologists, psychologists[100], sociologists and anthropologists so that a working sociolinguistic concept of ritual is very much required. Until only very recently, this area of communicative behaviour has been blatantly neglected by linguists who have not taken the sociocultural context of language into account apart from occasional, rather polemic, token references to ritual as conventionalized linguistic behaviour and who have been much more interested in the generation of creative and novel sentences.

When the linguistic dimensions of ceremoniousness have been treated it is the symbolic anthropologists of exotic societies who have generally referred to it in an unsystematic and untheoretical manner. Very recently, a new school of sociologists has begun to explore the significant amount of ritual involved in daily interaction (cf. Goffman 1967). German linguists have also shown interest in ritual language (cf. Werlen 1979, 1984), particularly its routine aspects such as in greetings (Hartmann 1973) and formulae (cf. Coulmas 1979, 1981b). In this study, however, ritual is identified less with conventional routines of interaction and more broadly with the collective linguistic performance and construction of ritual as a socio-cultural metaphor. To explain this, we shall have to venture into the abstract and theoretical realm of ritual.

Generally, ritual is not a conscious concept for its actors. The term does not usually belong to part of a folk taxonomy (Werlen 1979: 154). However, ritual as a specific, circumscribed social activity often bears names that point to its perception as a special ceremony e.g. *'funeral'* or *'namakke'*, a Cuna healing speech event (cf. Sherzer 1974), or *'nmaa dumɔ'*, a ritual for planting millet of the Ga in Ghana (cf. Fitzgerald 1975), or *'hirōen'*, a Japanese wedding-announcement gathering.

In fact these four cases all point to the multifunctional nature of ritual events of a collective kind: the *funeral* marks a life/death crisis; *namakke* is performed for therapeutic, magical effects; *nmaa dumɔ* expresses human dependency on nature and *hirōen* regularizes a status change. In fact, the reception can be interpreted as a kin rite de passage permitting the bride entry into her husband's household. At the same time, the Japanese word for 'bride': *shimpu* and for 'groom': *shinrō* mean literally 'new woman' and 'new man', thus also pointing to the sanctioned entry into new adult status[101]. From these events we can see how closely the notion of ritual is associated with the enactment and commitment to a particular belief-system.

For Malinowski (1961) the elaborate fishing-rituals of the Trobiand islanders served as a form of crisis management, a method of soothing anxieties before setting out into dangerous, open sea. Radcliffe-Brown (1965: 160), on the other hand, maintains that ritual is not a regulating response to a problem but rather the "regulated expression" of "certain human feelings and sentiments ... which, by their control of or influence on the conduct of individuals, made possible the existence and continuance of an orderly social life". In other words, rites are a response to problems of social structure so that our wedding reception, or example, could be interpreted as a social mechanism regulating the possibly antagonistic relationship between spouse and in-laws.

Actually, Durkheim (1972: 219-38) views the function of ritual in terms of its articulating values and principles and mobilizing the commitment of community members which is taken up by Leach (1976: 41): "We engage in ritual in order to transmit collective messages to ourselves".

Leaving the raison d'être for ritual, one finds that the communicative acts in ritual events have often been characterized as irrational. Firth (1972: 3) describes them as "formal procedures of a communicative but arbitrary kind" and Goody (1961: 159) refers to them as a "category of standardized behaviour (custom) in which the relationship between the means and end is not intrinsic". This lack of rationality claimed for the form of ritual acts is, of course, due to their often petrified nature: the motivation for their original creation is no longer transparent to their performers which may lead to such acts being negatively evaluated as empty conventions and meaningless formalities (cf. Coulmas' remarks (1979: 172)).

However, ritual is undeniably meaningful. We have seen how it provides a method of dealing with social anxiety and affirming the values and structure of a cultural system by setting up an apparently non-rational, symbolic framework. Thus, ritual here is taken as constituting a collective meta-communicative event[102] of societal-constructing significance.

2.2.1. *Ritual resources at the reception*

The ceremonial use of space and objects such as the golden screen has already been noted above. In the status-based turn-taking system of the reception speech-givers we can find regulated structuring of action which is a characteristic element of ritual. Other codes are also employed to construct ritual such as the various changes in costume and kinesics e.g. the standing posture of the bride and groom while listening to the first two speeches and the bride's lowered head and eyes throughout the reception as well as the groom's father's actual reference to the somber countenance he has to maintain during the proceedings.

But what are the fundamental linguistic components drawn upon to produce ritual? First of all, let us examine the contents of the eight speeches given at the reception. In fact, the master of ceremonies calls upon each speech giver to deliver *shukuji* 'a congratulatory address' and *aisatsu* 'a formal greeting', here undoubtedly of a congratulatory nature. These are the speech givers' folk conceptions of their speech events.

It is possible to divide the shukuji and aisatsu into a set of basic speech acts in the Hymesian sense (1972: 56)[103] and these are presented in Table 1.

To illustrate how these speech acts were abstracted from the reception shukuji and aisatsu, let us take the case of 'commending a person' (no.6. in Table 1) and exemplify this with extracts from speeches.

> *SG1*:   the groom's father "has an extremely wonderful personality and I always hold great respect for him. As for his established position of work, generally speaking, he was not involved with pottery originally but he has striven very hard alone and now in the Oroshi manufacturers' association of which there are about 200 members he produces the Hantsuki products and is the most outstanding of this group of producers".

> *SG4*: "if I speak frankly when I first met the bride it was the case that ... on first seeing her (I realized) how greatly she resembles her father. You could instantly recognize that she's his daughter. I'm sure her character entirely takes after the best elements in her father and mother".

These two comments have been reduced to the fundamental speech act of *commending a person* and the same principle applies to the other acts listed in Table 1 where SG1's speech acts have been taken as a pattern with which to compare the speech acts of the other shukuji givers. Of course, the table does not take the variation in sequencing of the acts into account. SG1's speech acts are presented in their order of occurrence against which the others' are marked off. But their sequencing does not seem to be at all significant for what emerges from Table 1 is that the most frequently repeated acts were self-introduction (no.1), thanking (no.4), explicating a particular relationship (no.5), appealing on behalf of the groom's household for subservience from the bride (no.7) and congratulating (no.10). It is also interesting to recognize how similar the speech givers' speech acts are and how the speech givers are oriented to a fixed set of speech act types. Moreover, these speech acts may be taken as *ritual routines*.

Most of the prominent speech acts (nos. 1,4,5,7 and 19) can be explained with reference to the context: explicating a particular relationship is necessary for validating a recommendation; a plea to the bride to integrate herself into her new household is bound up with traditional attitudes towards brides; thanking and congratulating are routines demanded by the event.

It is, of course, impossible to deal with all these ritual speech acts within the scope of this presentation but we shall focus on the first one: self-introduction.

It should be observed, first of all, that not every one of the speech givers

Table 1. *A Comparison of the Speech Givers' Speech Acts.* (The speech acts are marked by a cross if they occurred and a minus if they did not. More than one cross signifies repetition of the act).

SG1's SPEECH ACTS	SG2	SG3	SG4	SG5	SG6	SG7	SG8
self introduction	+	-	+	+	-	-	+
apologising	-	+	+++	-	-	-	-
promising short speech	+	+	-	-	-	-	-
thanking	+	++	+	++	-	-	++
explaining relations	+	-	+	+	++	+	+
commending someone	+	-	+++	-	++	-	-
appealing on behalf of of groom's household	+	++	-	+	+	-	-
appealing on behalf of bride	++	-	-	-	+	-	-
marking end of speech	+	-	+	+	-	-	-
congratulating	-	++	++	+++	-	++	-

performed the act of self introduction. This demonstrates that the ritual routines here are not obligatory norms of verbal conduct and that they may be forgotten or omitted. In this connection one should note that only five out of the eight speakers did any congratulating which is supposedly an indispensable routine in a congratulatory address.

All the acts of self introduction were accompanied by a brief lowering of the head and neck (*eshaku*). This movement signals the beginning of interaction. What is, however, eminently ritualistic here is the redundancy of the self introduction since every one of the five speakers performing self-introducing routines had been just introduced by the master of ceremonies. This reminds one of the irrational nature of ritual encoding referred to at the outset. In fact, for all but SG2, these prior introductions immediately preceded the speech givers' own repetitions of their names. Here is an example of the re-occurring redundancy:

MASTER OF CEREMONIES:

> Yamamoto   Masao sama yori hitokoto go-shukuji
> FAMILY NAME FIRST NAME from some words speech
> o chodai itashitai to zonjimasu. Yamamoto-sama,
> receive humbly   request   FAMILY NAME
> yoroshiku   o-negai itashimasu.
> accordingly favour   humbly ask

SG5:   Go-shimei itadakimashita. Yamamoto de gozaimasu.
        selection humbly received FAMILY NAME am

Thus, the name was invariably repeated three times in succession in an interval of thirty seconds. These superfluous self-introductions are, of course, closely linked to a general Japanese sensitivity for formalized procedure in interaction outside the intimate sphere. But they also relate to a further essential aspect of symbolic ritual, namely the focus on defining identities and roles. This point will be subsequently taken up, but it should be noted for the present how necessary the speech givers felt the explicit restating of their identities to be.

Next, let us turn from fixed speech acts to another significant element of ritual language — formulism. By this I mean all those conventional phrases a speech community employs in polite and non-polite situations which may or may not (depending on its resources) include greeting, leave-taking, cursing, congratulating, toasting, introducing etc. Certain formulae such as apologies, thanks, farewells, condolences and stumbles have been explained in terms of face-saving devices cf. Brown and Levinson (1978: 240), but it seems unlikely that sensitivity to face can explain all formulistic usage e.g. congratulating.

Our concern here, however, is not with the socio-evaluative semiotics of formulism[104] but with their contribution to rituality. When speakers employ formulae, they draw upon the community's well-known stock of fixed phrases and demonstrate recognizable familiarity with and loyalty to the community's code as well as implicitly to its values. These petrified forms relate and refer to a specific, historically given social framework. Adherence to this framework is expressed and partly achieved in the employment of formulae. This, in turn, contributes to the affirmation of the therein indexicalized social order.

In connection with this, if the conception of ritual as a collective metacommunicative event of societal-constructing significance is reconsidered, it becomes clearer why formulae are frequently considered as mini-rituals. Some examples of formulae occurring at the reception are listed in Table 2; they have been related to the act they set out to apologize for, termed a 'trigger'. In fact, there are many other types of formulae employed at the reception (appreciative, supplicatory, congratulatory etc.) but these can not all be treated here.

Interestingly enough, all the triggers for these apologetic formulae are acts of individual behaviour which impose on the collective. Furthermore, no attempt is made to personalize them; the act to which they refer is not even mentioned. This non-personalization and deixis are, of course, fundamental characteristics of Japanese formulistic usage. The abstract and impersonal nature of the formulae are further devices contributing to rituality. Individual and original means of expression have to be framed within declarations of conformity to fixed procedure; these conformist declarations are the formulae:

SG1 marks the opening of his speech with an apology for talking from the specially 'high' and separate position as 'go-between'; SG4 intends to end his with the same apologetic formulae but continues because he suddenly remembers that he has forgotten to mention the groom's family; the groom's father immediately utters the formula *domo go-burei itashimashita* after singing, which functions as a closing while the bank manager opens his toasting to the couple with an apologetic formula.

Not only as definers of interaction stages, these formulae also confirm the speakers' orientation to a collectively performed event and signal their commitment to its norms and values.

So far we have seen how ritual can be constructed out of fixed turn-taking, speech acts and formulism. We shall now focus less on this predeterministic verbal behaviour and more on the little discussed symbolization of

Table 2. *Apologetic Formulae occurring at the Reception.*

SPEAKER	FORMULA	TRIGGER
SG1/ SG4	shitsurei de gozaimasu rude am	high position as go-between/ long speech
groom's father	domo go-burei itashimashita very much rudeness done	singing
bank manager	senetsu de gozaimasu audacious am	proposing a toast

social distance occurring in ritual events.

That the 'tone of voice' of performers of ritual may be significant will come as no surprise. This aspect will not be pursued here but it is worth noting that the pitch of the older male speech-givers was judged to be markedly higher than the pitch they employed in daily interaction among colleagues and associates and intimates. Goffman's statement on ritual helps to elucidate this (1967: 57): "ritual ... represents a way in which the individual must guard or design the symbolic implications of his acts while in the immediate presence of an object that has a special value for him".

It is seems that the ritual-constituting 'object of value' that the participants are confronted with here is the occasion itself — *hirōen*. Thus, the deference assigned to the occasion is encoded in the use of extra high pitch which in Japanese may serve as a signal of respect giving cf. chapter 4.

However, apart from the prosodic and even phonological (in terms of standard Japanese pronunciation versus dialect) markers of ritual, there are also other linguistic dimensions to be explored.

In contemporary Japanese, there exists a range of address suffixes which can connote varying levels of social respect or distance and intimacy (cf. Fig.1). The fact that the suffix *san* can be crudely equated with Mr/Miss/Mrs is widely known. *San* is, in fact, a historical contraction of a much more deferential suffix, *sama*, which according to the prescriptive guidelines of the Japanese Ministry of Education should nowadays be reserved for address via the written channel or in certain fixed phrases or for formal occasions[105]. Actually, at the reception the master of ceremonies employs *sama* to designate almost every participant; even the groom's little nephew and niece are referred to as *o-ko-sama* (honorific prefix + child(ren) + honorific suffix), a style of address and reference that is highly deferential and unusual.

What interests us here is the reason why the honorific suffix *sama* can be and is used in "formal occasions". How can we account for the link between the linguistic symbolization of social distance and ritual?

The explanation offered here is that a linguistic norm of de-personalization or social distancing operates in ritual events. Through the superelevation of nearly every participant with the suffix *sama*, a sense of the separateness and uniqueness as well as the imputed 'high-ness' of the thus designated is achieved. The choice of *sama* has to be interpreted in relation to other alternative suffixes available for the children such as *chama* (diminutive honorific for children), *chan* (diminutive everyday suffix for children) and *san*, the first two of which could provide a more personalized and less socially distanced term of address.

However, syntactic devices are also employed to these ends as can be seen in the use of verbal honorifics at the reception. This system has already been briefly outlined (in ch.1. section 1.2.1. and notes 13-16) and here we shall see how verbal honorifics connoting social distance signal ritual. Our first example derives from the second speech at the reception given by the bride's male go-between who is the cousin of the bride's father. One normative constraint on Japanese honorific usage generally is that it should not be used to refer to one's own in-group in interaction with an outgroup member: the outgroup should be respectfully raised while one's in-group humbled. However, SG2 violates this norm, as many of the other speakers, by employing extremely elevating forms for his cousin:

| | | 1 | 2 | 3 |

o-tōsan ga ... Kagawa-ken no hō ni _go_-tenkin ni nari-
mashita
father   subj. marker NAME of prefecture of direction transferred
1. HONORIFIC PREFIX+ 2 REFERENT + 3 ADDRESSEE HONORIFIC

To refer to his cousin's transfer by his company to a different prefecture in Japan, SG2 employs the honorific prefix _go-_ and the referent honorific verb form _ni naru_. In the same speech he also refers with an honorific passive form[106] to the bride who is, of course, much younger and sociolinguistically usually his inferior. In his ordinary interaction, SG1 would not honorifically raise the bride in this manner but speak to her in neutral forms i.e. not honorific language. On the other hand, the bride speaks up to her elderly male relative and employs mild referent honorifics without the addressee morpheme honorific _masu_.

In other words, the speaker of these utterances separates himself from his own relatives in referring to them at the reception. In the performance of ritual events, actors attempt therefore to achieve a de-individualized state where identities relating to ego are submerged and extrinsically circumscribed. This emphasis on the extrinsic is, of course, connected to the commitment to outer requirements i.e. that which is collective.

So far the characteristic lexical flavour of ritual language has not been considered. It is common knowledge that 'old fashioned' forms are frequently employed in ceremonious events. These archaisms are linked to the commitment to 'the way things have always been done', that is to say, tradition. An alluminating illustration of this is provided at the reception by the master of ceremonies when he introduces the seventh speech-giver:

Soredewa suzukimashite/ shinrō no go-yūjin de irasshaimasu/
So we shall continue/   we have a friend of the groom/

Takahashi   Junichi-sama yori hitokoto o-spīchi e...
from Mr Takahashi Juniichi I would like to humbly request a
o-iwai no o-kotoba chōdai   itadakereba to omoimasu ga /
speech er... congratulatory address/

Takahashi-sama   irasshaimasen ka? Sumimasen/
Is Mr Takahashi here?   Excuse me.

What has happened here is that the loan word *o-spīchi* 'speech' has slipped out and is immediately replaced by the less contemporary sounding term, *o-iwai no kotoba* 'congratulatory address'. This is the first (and last) occasion the master of ceremonies employs the lexeme *spīchi* and the reason for its occurrence can only be conjectured: perhaps it is due to the increased informal and modern tone of the second half of the reception or maybe the younger age of the seventh speech giver in contrast to those up until that moment provoked a 'younger' and more 'modern' association for the master of ceremonies. Whatever the cause for the style-switch, it is very significant that it was perceived as a violation and corrected. By re-employing the native synonym, the master of ceremonies once again proves that a basic component of linguistic ritual is the adherence to a historical, traditional code which is less associated with individualized communicative styles. This de-emphasis on the personal has been referred to in the definition of ritual as a *collective* metacommunicative event of societal-constructing significance.

Let us conclude then by reviewing what has been learnt. The occasion was constructed linguistically out of the following components:
– pre-established turns
– fixed speech acts, e.g. the reoccurrence of similar speech acts in Table 2
– redundancy, e.g. the act of self-introduction
– formulism, e.g. semantically empty but diachronically valued and preserved phraseology
– social extrinsicality, e.g. the general use of the address suffix -*sama* and verbal referent honorifics for ingroup members while addressing an outgroup
– archaic or tradition-oriented lexis, i.e. the avoidance of modernisms

From this it is evident that the linguistic devices associated with ceremoniousness lay a premium on non-egocentric, collectively pre-determined, traditional patterns of verbal behaviour.

Thus, ritual language is not as irrational as some have maintained. The findings presented here seem in retrospect to correlate with Durkheim's statement (1972: 219-238) on ritual as the occasion when the primacy of society is realized, when the adherence to its values is articulated and affirmed. Here it has been shown how the language of a ritual event metaphorically signals participants' commitment to their social system and celebrates that commitment in a manner which can be called 'sacred' which, according to the Oxford English Dictionary, can mean "consecrated to; esteemed especially dear or acceptable to a deity" and "dedicated, set apart, exclusively appropriated to some person or some *special purpose*". At the reception the exclusive consecration is not to a deity or person but to the "special purpose" of society as represented by the assembled guests.

2.3. Hierarchical and collective signals: the contextual dynamics of designatory forms

Up to now studies of address systems (cf. Brown and Gilman 1960, Ervin-Tripp 1969, Friedrich 1972, Bates and Benigni 1975 and Haugen 1975) have typically concentrated on either correlating linguistic forms with social characteristics based on scales of superiority and distance, or tracing the historical development of address forms, or providing a predictive description of contemporary address rules. Although such indexical aspects of address systems are undeniably worth investigating, such research is, as Dittmar (1976: 109) points out: "oriented towards superficial categories ... which do not explain the actual conditions reflected in address forms". Moreover, though the classic question of the causal relationship between language and culture is still unresolved, the mainstream of sociolinguistic research still seems dangerously uninterested in the ethnophilosophical forces underlying speech.

In order to account more adequately for address behaviour and accompanying forms, I hope to show here how profitable can be the adoption of an ethnographic perspective whereby the speech community's set of social norms, attitudes, and beliefs is viewed as an ongoing process of linguistic encoding of social concepts. It should become obvious from the ensuing argument that certain aspects of linguistic form and behaviour can only be explicated by direct reference to the social organisation, value system and the "social reality" of the community itself (cf. Sapir 1929: 209). In order to do this, we shall look at Japanese forms of address and reference, here termed designatory markers, as they occurred in the wedding speeches.

In Japanese, terms of address and reference are frequently the same since pronouns such as 'he', 'she', 'they', are generally avoided for reasons of politeness unless explications of the referent is necessary (cf. ch.1. section 1.2.2.). Instead of pronouns, the Japanese prefer names, titles, kin and role terms[107], or equally frequently, avoid all direct reference and produce ellipsis (cf. Hinds 1982a). The term 'designatory markers' has been chosen here to cover these various forms and also to include honorific forms (which may be verbal constructions) since terms of address and reference belong to the same category of linguistic phenomena in Japanese.

First of all, those markers uttered in the opening section of the first reception speech will be focussed upon. Here is a transcription of the beginning section of the speech with an accompanying translation which is as literal as possible:

1. *Suzuki Chiba go-ryōke no baishaku no go-en o emashita no de/*
   Because I've been given the opportunity to be a go-between for the
2. *hanahada takai tokoro kara shitsurei de gozaimasu ga/*
   Suzuki and Chiba households/please forgive me for (speaking) from this
3. *hitokoto go-aisatsu o mōshiagemasu/*
   extremely high position/ but I will only say a few words/
4. *honjitsu wa heijitsu de arimashite/nanika to taihen no naka/*
   today (even though) a week day/ inspite of this very busy time/
5. *kōgyōkumiai no rijichōsan o hajime dairi no minasamagata ni wa*
   I wish to deeply thank, first of all, the president of the manufac-
6. *taihen o-isogashī naka o magete, shinrō shimpu no shukufuku ni*
   turers' association and those who have come in the place of others in
7. *go-rinseki tamawarimashite, makoto ni arigatō gozaimashita/*
   spite of this very busy period and honoured us with their attendance
8. *atsuku onrei mōshiagemasu/*
   to give blessings to the groom and bride once again I express thanks/
9. *Suzuki-ke to watashi to wa sanjūnenrai no go-kōsai de gozaimashite/*
   the Suzuki household and I have been acquainted for thirty years/
10. *Suzuki-san wa kōgyōkumiai no yakuin/*
    and Mr Suzuki is a representative of the manufacturers' association/
11. *gakkō no fukukaichō/ chōnai no yakuin/*
    deputy president of the PTA/representative of the neighbourhood assoc.
12. *to go-issho ni yarimashita keredomo/hijō ni jinkaku no rippa na kata*
    and we served on these together/ (he) has an extremely wonderful

13. *de/watakushi wa itsumo sonkei shite oru mon' de arimasu/*
    personality/and I always hold great respect for him/

14 *shokuba ni okimashite wa/ichiō tōki to zenzen kankei*
    as for his established position at work/ generally speaking, he was not

15 *no nai kata de arimashita keredomo/ jibun ni doryoku saremashite/*
    involved in pottery (originally)/but he strove very hard alone/ and

16 *genzai dewa Arashi no kōgyōkumiai demo 200 kenchikaku arimasu*
    now in the Arashi manufacturers' association of which there are about

17. *keredomo /Hantsuki seihin to shite wa saiyūshū no shuryoku ni*
    200 members/ he produces the Hantsuki products and is the best person

18 *arareru kata de arimashite/watakushi wa tsunezune sonkei o mōshiagete*
    among the leaders/ I have always respected him very much/

19 *orimasu/Kōrei ni yorimashite/shinrō no go-shōkai o itashimasu/shinrō*
    As customary/ I shall now introduce the groom/ Groom

20 *Ryūchi-kun wa Shōwa 24-nen rokugatsu 23-nichi ni Suzuki-ke no jinan*
    Ryūichi was born in the 24th year of the Showa period on the 23rd

21 *to shite tanjō shi/...*
    July as the second son of the Suzuki household/.

The above transcript is an extempore piece of speech-giving from the male go-between for the groom, who starts by showing respect to both households in the marriage. It is interesting that the groom's household, Suzuki by name, is placed before the bride's, Chiba, in line 1. This seems to indicate that by naming it first, priority is assigned to the male partner's household. A similar sequencing occurs in line 6: the word for 'groom' *shinrō* precedes 'bride' *shimpu*. These two instances can be brought into connection with the denial of speaking rights to the central female participants already discussed above (under section 2.1.1.).

Furthermore, in line 1 there is an honorific prefix *go-* in front of the word for 'both households' *ryōke* which elevates the status of the two groups above the speaker's. Interestingly, the speaker himself had been introduced by the master of ceremonies at the reception as *go-baishaku* (honorific prefix + 'go-between'), but when he refers to his role as go-between, again in line 1, we can observe that the prefix *go-*, is not employed for self-reference. This is an example of the recurring constraint of linguistically marked status.

To understand how the speakers dynamically adapt designatory markers to create and suit a social reality, let us now turn to line 5-6, where the speaker mentions his gratitude, first of all, not to the couple nor their parents for inviting him, but to the president of the pottery manufacturers' association (of which the speaker is a member) for deigning to attend the reception on a busy weekday. Ranking is indicated by topic placing.

The speaker refers to the association's president as *kōgyōkumiai no rijichōsan* 'manufacturers' association + of + president + *san*'. *San* is a general designatory suffix which, according to the prescriptive pronouncements of the Japanese National Language Research Institute should only follow names and kin terms but not titles since the latter, such as 'president' here, are already honorific enough. The speaker's addition of *san* after *rijichō* is a highly deferential form of designation. Moreover, the manufacturers' association is a voluntarily formed group of independent businessmen with its president being elected. Why then the apparent obsequiousness? The speaker commented later that it was difficult to explain exactly why he was so extra-polite here but it seemed that standing in front of all the people in the hall he felt it necessary to show special appreciation to the president.

The contextual factors involved here are complex. Designatory markers are not simply used to identify and categorize individuals within a particular sociocultural framework. They also assume a polyvalent function, and in this example we can see how they can be influenced by — as well as indexicalize — the speaker's interpretation of the setting (formal/informal) and of the nature of the message (here: thanking).

Later in line 10, the speaker refers to the groom's father by surname + *san*: *Suzuki-san*, which is the most neutral of designatory suffixes in Japanese. The last *san* is in no way comparable to the one occurring after 'president' above because it follows a name and not a title. However, a little later in the speech (line 20) the speaker refers to the groom by first name + *kun*: *Ryūchi-kun*. *Kun* is a designatory suffix for males, often young males such as students or boys in the same group, class, or club who may use it reciprocally as comrades or may be thus addressed by older and superior males cf. the use of the second person singular pronoun in European languages.

The groom would never address his go-between with *kun*, as it would constitute a presupposed equality that cannot exist because of age and social network differences (the go-between is an associate of the groom's father). Although the speaker maintained in a later interview that he was really only expressing comradeship by addressing the groom with *kun*, he was, in fact, adhering to an age-based hierarchy, because the use of *kun* was not reciprocal. Similar to this question of *kun*, there is later in the same speech a reference to the bride as *Etsuko-san*. This, of course, is not the usual form of address by the speaker for the bride since first naming is reserved only for close relatives and friends, usually from childhood. The first speaker is in no way related to the bride's family. His designation of her with first name here is due to a special "imaginative" position whereby the speaker has adopted the viewpoint of the husband who will address his wife by first name. The speech-giver here is echoing the address patterns of the future partners in marriage which functions as a means of bringing them closer to the audience and countering feelings of distance. However, it is only a temporary phenomenon that is restricted to this one context.

What we have seen so far is how the meaning of designatory markers can only be derived from analyzing the participants' active manipulation and reaction to the entire situation. The wedding reception is not merely the enactment of an established social framework but, as these examples demonstrate, the constitution of a new one which is dynamically symbolized in the selection of designatory forms.

The organization of speaking as seen in the turn-taking and distribution of rights to the floor and the structuring of utterances, such as with these designatory markers, both reveal the participants' accomplished representation of a rank-based hierarchy, with the groom's household taking precedence over the bride's, the guest speakers assuming priority over both households, older males over younger ones, and males over females. The important point here is not that the statuses set up by the designatory markers refer to an external, societal categorization but that the participants in the wedding reception have created these statuses by means of their linguistic contributions and co-produced the social reality.

Further examples of the linguistic symbolization of hierarchically ordered status could be provided by investigating the honorific verbal constructions of the speech above, but instead let us turn to another dimension of designatory marking which throws light on linguistic indexing here: how the forms are employed to signal collective belonging.

If we study the data presented in Table 3 which show the designatory markers for the groom offered during the reception, it is noticeable that none of the speech givers from the groom's household ever designate the groom with a suffix more respectful than *kun*. In contrast to this, the bride's representative never omit a suffix nor use *kun* to designate the groom; speaker 4 never fails to place *san* after *shinrō*, thereby marking his respect for the groom. Similarly, speakers 4 and 6 refer to the groom as *o-muko-san* (honorific prefix + *san* + honorific suffix). This doubly polite designation indi-

SPEECH GIVER	Designatory forms for the groom
SG6, SG4	o-muko-san 'son'
master of ceremonies	o-nī-chan 'elder brother'
SG4, master	shinrō-san 'groom'
SG4	hanamuko-san 'groom'
SG1	shinro Ryūichi-kun 'groom' + first name
SG5, bank manager	Ryūichi-kun first name
SG7	Suzuki-kun last name
SG6	Suzuki-san last name
SG5, SG1	shinrō 'groom'

Table 3. Designatory markers for the groom occurring at the reception.

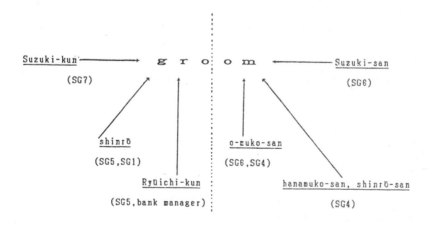

Fig. 3   Corporate identification in designatory markers for the groom

cates the extent to which the speakers from the bride's side have identified themselves as belonging to a separate and lower-placed group in relation to the groom.

It is not just unfamiliarity with the groom that accounts for this respectful affixing from the bride's speakers: the branch manager of a bank in Toki city had never met the groom before, and yet he referred to him by first name + *kun*, clearly marking through the intimate suffix their mutual belonging.

In this connection we should remember the obvious symbolization of corporate identification achieved by the seating arrangements for the reception, with two households separated on either side of the hall. Additionally, it is worth considering the group ties recognizable in the composition of the guests attending the reception. Nearly every guest who is not tied by blood to the newly-weds is related to the couple or their parents by some economic or social bond resulting from membership in a particular group. There are the seven members of the pottery manufacturers' association of which the groom's father is a member. The speech giver representing the groom comes from his own age groups: they were both students at the same high school and university. It should also be noted that employees of the groom's ceramics company had also been invited to the reception — which further underlines the importance of work ties. The use of honorific verbs at the reception also points to this collective aligning, but even though these are also forms of designatory marking, their full consideration is beyond the scope of this chapter.

Thus, there exist in every speech community certain sociocultural beliefs and values which are operative in linguistic behaviour and which come to be constructed in context. Here we have focussed only on how status ordering and corporate identification are expressed, observed, alluded to and actually constituted via designatory markers. We also see that such markers are polyfunctional, their 'meaning' and motivation deriving from the entire contextual matrix in which they are uttered. It should be noted that various non-verbal aspects of the reception, such as spatial semiotics, as well as discourse organization such as turn-taking, have been referred to in order to explain and arrive at a fuller understanding of the dynamics of designatory forms.

It should be clear that even such apparently circumscribed elements of language as designatory markers are inseparably bound to the participants' amalgamated management and accomplishment of social activity. When the sociocultural reality encoded and actively symbolized in speech behaviour is analysed, simplification, generalization and abstraction from the speech event are consequential and inevitable. Nevertheless, without the existence of cultural principles to guide interaction, the patterns of interaction themselves could scarcely be conducted or acquired.

2.4. A concluding note

From the discussion above, it should be obvious that certain aspects of linguistic form and use can only be adequately accounted for if they are both analysed in terms of the social structure and value system of the speech community which employs them. Inversely, such an ethnographic analysis can at the same time provide a guide to the social reality of the speech community. Although no one has so far been able to absolutely 'prove' the link between language and culture, it is undeniably within the area of *language use*, rather than grammar, that the interplay and interdependence of language and culture most forcefully emerge.

3. SPEAKING OF GIVING: THE PRAGMATICS OF JAPANESE DONATORY VERBS

This chapter shows the impossibility of applying a purely structuralist and transformationalist approach when accounting for a set of lexical and morphological items in Japanese, all of which relate to the one English sememe *give*. It also explores various syntactic, semantic and pragmatic frameworks to see which, if any, of these is capable of handling the data.

Donatory forms play an important role in the Japanese language: they are employed in making requests and orders, e.g. *doa o akete kudasai* (lit. door + object marker, opening give to me) which is equivalent to 'please open the door' and they also feature in a special set of constructions termed benefactives which express favours, e.g. *ano hito wa tegami o kaite kudasatta* (lit. that person letter writing gave to me) which may be translated as 'he wrote a letter for me'. Furthermore, because they belong to the area of honorifics, differentiating between types of givers and receivers, they require no overt reference to speaker, person spoken of or to — that is to say, pronouns in Indo-European languages. It is also important to note that certain donatory verbs function as referent honorifics[108], e.g. *sashiageru* and *kudasaru*. As just mentioned, there exist in Japanese various morphological and lexical forms to express the notion of 'giving': *ageru, sashiageru, o-age ni naru, o-age suru, o-age itasu, sashiagerareru, yaru, o-yari ni naru, kudasaru* and *kureru*[109] among others. There also exist other forms but these may be considered as either reserved for particular stylistic purposes or restricted to certain social or regional groups.

The choice between these various forms depends on the interpersonal relations perceived to hold between the giver and receiver, between speaker and giver and receiver and between hearer, giver and receiver. If the giver (G) has no relation to the speaker or the speaker's group, then the forms are as those shown in Diagram 1. As Lebra (1976: 22) observes, "the reference group varies widely from small to large, intimate to impersonal, formal to informal. It may be one's household, residential area, village or town, the company or factory where one works, the nation, and so forth". In the diagram the direction of the arrows from the receiver (R) indicates the social distance, status, or position believed or implied for G so that if it is higher than G, it implies higher status and if lower, a lower social position.

Thus, each of the forms may be considered as socially 'loaded' since they imply a particular social relationship or role. In fact, Miller (1971: 619) dismisses the view that honorifics are merely a system of connotations and instead sees them as firmly fixed within the whole linguistic system.

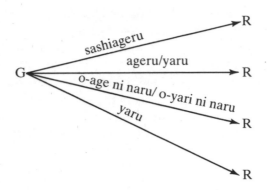

Diagram 1. Donatory froms where G is not the speaker nor belongs to the speaker's ingroup.

Here are examples of how the forms shown in diagram 1 may be employed.

    (1)   a. The student *gives* the teacher a camera.
          b. G ga R ni kamera o *sashiageru*[110].
    (2)   a. The man *gives* his friend a camera.
          b. G ga R ni kamera o *ageru*.
          c. G ga R ni kamera o *yaru*.

The choice between *ageru* and *yaru* is basically dependent on the level of politeness required for R. If R is to be respected then *ageru* is appropriate. There also seems to be a sex-linked restriction operating on *yaru*: as it has acquired a rough and even rude connotation (when describing the act of giving to a human being), it tends to be avoided by females who are expected to speak more politely in Japan (cf. Ch.1. section 1.3.2.1.).

    (3)   a. The teacher gives the student a camera.

    b. G ga R ni kamera o *o-yari ni naru*.
    c. G ga R ni kamera o *o-age ni naru*.
    d. G ga R ni kamera o *yaru*.

Here (3)b. and c. considerably elevate the giver while d. sharply derogates the receiver.

The potential subjectivity of the semantic selection of Japanese donatory forms where the speaker brings his personal involvement, previous experience and perceptual information among other factors into his determination of the appropriate form should now be obvious. It is, of course, related to the field of 'social deixis' which refers to the dependence of a linguistic item on the context of who is speaking to whom or about whom i.e. "that aspect of sentences which reflect or establish or are determined by certain realities of the social situation in which the speech act occurs" (Fillmore 1975: 7).

Social deixis exists covertly in English in cases such as (4) below.

(4)   a. You must have some of this cake.
       b. You should have some of this cake.
       c. You may have some of this cake.
    (Lakoff 1972: 910)

The variation in sentence (4) depends on an awareness of the social status of other conversation participants. The importance of the relationship between speaker and addressee can also be gauged from the degrees of politeness expressed in the orders of sentence (5).

(5)   a. Come in, won't you?
       b. Please come in.
       c. Come in.
       d. Come in, will you?
       e. Get the hell in here!
    (Lakoff 1972: 914)

However, the distinction between socially deictic and socially non-deictic usages of donatory forms is not always transparant. There is no deixis where the social ranking of giver and receiver has been made explicit in the sentence as in (1), (2) and (3) above, for social convention determines these cases. For instance, in sentence (3) we are presented with adequate indications concerning the relative status of giver and receiver: because a student is conventionally considered (in Japanese society) as 'lower' than his teacher, his teacher is expected to 'give downward' to him, the social assymetry being expressed in the forms *o-yari ni naru, o-age ni naru* and *yaru*. Where no explicit reference to the status of givers and receivers can be found within the utterance, the extralinguistic context becomes all-decisive and social deixis arises. Clearly, no speaker possesses any kind of absolute status since address by an intimate would always shift this. Thus, the deictic nature of donatory forms arises from their being a linguistic expression of an assumed relationship between a particular giver and a particular receiver at a particular moment. Even, more deictally, whenever someone alludes to a relationship with a donatory form (or some other social symbol for that matter) he may impose his own, personal interpretation on its patterning for a variety of reasons such as politeness, flattery, rudeness, humour etc.

Thus, the *gave* in the sentence "The man gave the book to the teacher" would be socially deictic in Japanese; if the form for *gave* was *sashiageta* we would still not be any wiser about the status of the man in the sentence in relation to other people. All we would know would be his relation to this one particular teacher. Similarly, if *ageta* was selected, it would imply that the man was on a roughly equal basis to his teacher but provide no guide to his social position with regard to other givers and receivers. Obviously, what is required to generate acceptable utterances with donatory verbs are continuing indications of the relationship patterning between those involved. Social deixis arises when such social information is only available to a specific speaker in a specific context.

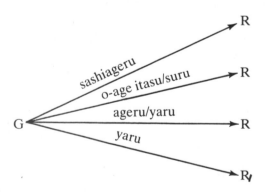

Diagram 2: Donatory forms where G is the speaker or in the speaker's group.

Now we will extend the presentation of the data further so that it includes those situations where the speaker and his group become givers, as shown in diagram 2.

From diagram 2 we can construct the following:

(6) a. I *give* the child a camera (where G is higher than R).
     b. G ga R ni kamera o *yaru*.
(7) a. My daughter *gives* the university lecturer a camera (where G is lower than R).
     b. G ga R ni kamera o *sashiageru*.
     c. G ga R ni kamera o *o-age suru*.
     d. G ga R ni kamera o *o-age itasu*[111].

Sentence (7)c. exalts R more than (7)b. because an object honorific or self-deprecating form has been employed, while (7)d. is even more self-humbling than (7)c., because *itasu* is a suppletive object honorific for *suru*, thus implying greater deference to R.

Completely different verb forms are employed when the recipient is the speaker or any of those associated with him cf. Diagram 3. One of these (*kudasaru*) is a subject honorific which raises the giver's status.

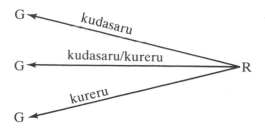

Diagram 3. Donatory forms where R is the speaker or in the speaker's group.

(8)   a. The teacher *gives* my brother a camera.
      b. G ga R ni kamera o *kudasaru*.
(9)   a. My friend gives me a camera.
      b. G ga R ni kamera o *kureru*.
      c. G ga R ni kamera o *kudasaru*[112].
(10) a. The child *gives* my aunt a camera.
      b. G ga R ni kamera o *kureru*.
(11) a. The teacher *gives* my aunt a camera.
      b. G ga R ni kamera o *ageru*.

The variation between (10)b. and (11)b. is due to the different focus adopted by the speaker: if the speaker has already spoken about the teacher and wishes to adopt a position from the teacher's perspective, he will use (11)b. If, however, the speaker wants to emphasize his affiliation with an ingroup member (here: his aunt) and thereby stress the receiving element of the action, he may choose (10)b. A further factor seems to be the level of presumed intimacy. If a speaker feels close enough to the receiver e.g. where he is living in the same house as the relative or has frequent contact with him/her, *kureru/kudasaru* will probably be selected more often than *ageru/yaru*. Exactly which forces come into play here requires further investigation[113]. The importance of speaker perspective is reflected in situations where both giver and receiver are related to the speaker. Thus Kuno (1973: 135) maintains that even if the receiver is closer to the speaker than the giver, *kureru/ kudasaru* cannot be used if R is "still not close enough to the speaker". However, if both G and R, as seen in sentence (12) below are close to the speaker, then it is a question of who is closer out of G and R to the speaker that determines the form.

(12) a. The teacher *gives* my friend some whisky.
      b. Sensei ga tomodachi ni uiskī o *ageru*.
      c. *Sensei ga tomodachi ni uiskī o *kudasaru*.
      (A star at the beginning of a sentence indicates a state of anomaly.)

(12)c. is anomalous because the speaker would not normally identify so closely with his friend as to mark him as a member of an ingroup in this context. A similar kind of problem occurs in (13) and (14).

(13) a. My aunt *gives* my brother some chocolates.
      b. Obasan ga otōto ni chokoreito o *kudasaru*.
(14) a. My brother *gives* my aunt some chocolates.
      b. Otōto ga obasan ni chokoreito o *ageru* (*kudasaru*).

Kuno (1973) states his inability to account for sentences like (14) where R is obviously a close member of the speaker's group and yet does not full into the *kureru/kudasaru* set. Clearly, one's aunt is of higher status and more distant than one's brother. What seems, therefore, to have taken place is a rejection of the forms indicating ingroup receiving and the adoption of those donatory forms for outgroup receivers as shown in diagram 1 and 2. This can be accounted for by establishing that there is a hierarchy within the ingroup which mirrors the hierarchy without. Whether the social scaling of the ingroup and outgroup is a task for general linguistics or sociolinguistics is open to question[114] and will be discussed shortly. Whatever the domain it is relegated to, acknowledgement of the existence of ingroup as well as outgroup hierarchies is vital if a grammar is going to generate and interpret sentences containing donatory forms on the basis of native-speaker intuitions.

As the pragmatic constraint of hearer influence, distinct from reference influence, seems restricted with regard to donatory forms[115] we will adopt the framework suggested above which deals with the hearer only indirectly in terms of inference. Of course, the essential criterion for deciding between the *kureru* and *ageru* sets within the ingroup depends generally on focus or the adoption of a giver's or receiver's 'outlook' as illustrated in the explanation for the difference between sentences (10)b. and (11)b.

Whenever there is a mixed bundle of receivers, even when some receivers are closely associated with the speaker, *ageru* is used unless the first person singular is included among the receivers. Compare (16) and (17):

(16) a. The child *gives* the mayor and MY FATHER some flowers.
      b. Kodomo ga shichōsan to CHICHI ni hana o *ageru*.
(17) a. The child *gives* the mayor, my father and ME and some other people some flowers.
      b. Kodomo ga shichōsan to chichi to WATASHI to hoka no hito ni hana o *kureru*.

From the above presentation of data, it is patent that any grammar of Japanese must be able to account for the non-deictic usages of donatory verbs, i.e. where there exist conventionalized absolutes of social ranking (cf. Gazdar (1978: 9), "A model of language production which randomly selects from such a set on an occasion of reference will clearly be missing something".)

(18) Miss Z *gives* the dog a bone (*yaru*).
(19) Mr X. *gives* the mayor/professor/company president a camera. (*sashiageru*).
(20) A girl *gives* her aunt/older brother/friend a camera (*ageru.*)

Apart from non-deictic usages, a grammar must also account for the social deixis occurring in sentences (21) to (23) below. As discussed above these cases arise from the inability of the grammar to decide autonomously without reference to the context on the status of givers in relation to receivers and vice versa. It is the contextual circumstances alone which determine the appropriateness of the donatory form.

(21) Mr[116] Tanaka *gives* a book to my brother (*kureru/kudasaru?*)
(22) A friend gives David a camera (*kureru[117]/kudasaru[117]/yaru/ageru/ o-yari ni naru/sashiagerareru/o-age itasu?*)
(23)   I give you a camera (*yaru/ageru/o-age itasu/sashiageru?*)

Whatever 'base form' is postulated, it will not be free from social connotations or implications. If *ageru* were selected on the basis of its implied equality and neutrality, sentences such as (24) would be anomalous because Japanese culture does not consider dogs as social equals.

(24) a. I *give* the dog a bone.
      b. *Inu ni hone o *ageru*.

Similarly, when addressing a superior *ageru* is considered inappropriate and, if uttered, open to various interpretations such as anger, bad manners, humour, irony etc.

We turn now to the question of how the data presented above may be handled. We begin with the syntactic framework proposed by Harada (1975: 500) who maintains that "the occurrence of an honorific form is, by and large, conditioned by grammatical factors". Harada takes the notion of social superiority[118] and with an optional transformation introduces an honorific form whenever an NP has been assigned an SSS which signifies a person socially superior to the speaker by encapsulating the predicate between the morphemes *o...ni naru* or *o ... suru*. Subject honorifics result from an NP subject marked SSS and object honorifics from a direct or indirect object NP, wherever that NP has been assigned an SSS. This framework only deals with honorific forms and therefore, cannot, of course, account for giving to inferiors since honorifics express the relationship between the speaker or his group members and superiors. Nevertheless, this is no major defect and this could be easily remedied in purely grammatical terms by introducing an SIS which would represent a subject socially inferior to the speaker and an SES representing a subject socially equal to the speaker. An SBS representing a subject socially belonging to the speaker would also have to be introduced to differentiate between the *kureru* and *ageru* sets. Let us look at an example of how Harada's account could be applied to donatory forms.

(25) a. The teacher gave the student a camera.
      b. Sensei ga gakusei ni kamera o *? -ru*.

No base form is postulated in (25) b. (which Harada would have to do) because of the objections raised on the basis of sentences (18) to (24).

(25) c. Deep structure:

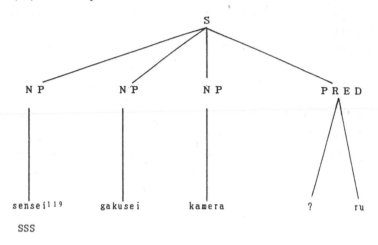

(25) d. After transformation:

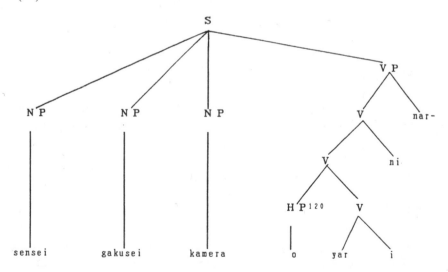

    The problem which arises in (25) is that we have no mechanism for relating *gakusei* (student) to *sensei* (teacher) but only a mechanism for relating *sensei* to the speaker in terms of the SSS feature. Thus, an honorific form may be generated but there is no provision made for selection between donatory forms. In other words, there is no way that the grammar here can choose between *ageru* and *yaru* and decide which is the appropriate form for a particular situation.

Another problem lies in restricting NP's that can take an SSS (or SIS). It is considered inappropriate to elevate a member of one's own family in contexts where one is speaking to someone outside one's family group. Thus, sentence (26) would be considered anomalous in all contexts — unless it was an intentional violation for humorous or sarcastic purposes because younger brothers conventionally never receive honorific respect.

(26) a.　Dr Yamada *gives* a book to my younger brother.
　　　 b.　*Yamada sensei ga otōto ni hon o *o-age suru*.

Here it is the indirect object that has been assigned as SSS (*otōto*), creating an object honorific. Even if all lexical entries were marked whether or not they could take an SSS or not, how could the grammar alone distinguish between (27)b. and (28)b. where a lexeme takes [+/− SSS]?

(27) a.　Dr Yamada *gives* the child a book.
　　　 b.　Yamada sensei ga kodomo ni hon o *o-yari ni naru*.
　　　　　 + SSS　　　　　　　　　　− SSS
(28) a.　Dr Yamada *gives* the child a book.
　　　 b.　Yamada sensei ga kodomo ni hon o *o-age itasu*.
　　　　　 + SSS　　　　　　　　　　+ SSS

In (27) the child is related neither to the speaker nor to the addressee and is definitely inferior to Dr. Yamada, hence *yaru* in honorific form. However, if in a particular context, the child referred to was the Emperor's for example, and the speaker considered showing respect to a member of the imperial family more important than to Dr Yamada, the object honorific *o-age itasu* might be chosen. Harada makes no attempt to deal with this contextualization of SSS features which not only means that (28)b. cannot be generated in his analysis but also that it is left unexplicated.

Additionally, rules will have to be set up to block the honorific transformation whenever an SSS subject or object co-occurs with reference to the first person as in (29), a phenomenon linked to the restriction on ingroup 'elevation' mentioned earlier.

(29) a.　The child *gives* the mayor and my father some flowers.
　　　 b.　Kodomo ga shichōsan to chichi ni hana o *ageru*.
　　　　　　　　　　 + SSS

c. *Kodomo ga shichōsan to chichi ni hana o *o-age itasu*.
+ SSS

If a grammar of a language is an explicit description of an ideal speaker's intrinsic competence (Chomsky 1965: 4), then the above restrictions must be explicated because they obviously form part of the system which underlies sentence production. The question raised here is how a grammer can assess an *ideal* speaker's social relationships. Who is the ideal speaker for donatory forms? How does he/she relate to *teacher*, *child*, *mayor* or anybody else? Whatever the answer is, it cannot be that the ideal speaker is neutral. It would be very strange to have two sentences showing this ideal speaker equal to dogs and children (through the use of *ageru*) in one sentence and equal to the mayor and a university professor in another in a Japanese context!

A related problem is that of data idealization. Harada points out that the degree of 'honorification' varies from speaker to speaker (1975: 547). In fact, donatory forms such as *o-age ni naru* are not employed by most Japanese in everyday life. Thus, it should now be clear that Harada's framework is unable to handle the deictic element of donatory verbs because he fails to provide machinery to assign an SSS to an NP, believing that "all ... a grammatical description has to say is that a predicate is put in the subject honorific form if its subject denotes an SSS" (1975: 501). But we have seen that there must be considerable restrictions on the SSS transformations in order to block inappropriate honorification and that the constraints on these selectional restrictions are context-dependent, and therefore impossible to state in a grammar which takes no account of context.

As Makino (1970) rejects the purely syntactic approach to honorifics he first proposes in his paper, we shall not discuss it here. The reason for this rejection was that transformation of every sentential element into an honorific form results in abnormal Japanese that would be considered unacceptable in most contemporary situations. Makino's first proposal is to set up transformations based on the [+/− POLITE] feature which does not differ, in principle, from Harada's SSS transformations: both frameworks restructure morphemes on the basis of a particular politeness feature. Likewise, Prideaux (1970: 59) introduces "politeness concord" in base rules while "transformations provide the proper affixes and periphrastic constructions which are manifestations of the concord".

Before we enter a further discussion on semantic-type restrictions on honorification, we must recognize that donatory forms involve both syntactic operations such as prefixing a verbal stem with *o* and suffixing either *ni naru* or *suru* or *itasu* and semantic operations which involve choice of appropriate lexical item[122]. Failure to observe selectional rules can result in the anomalies we shall leave open, but from any viewpoint they are ill-formed. However, honorific inappropriateness does not depend solely on the properties assigned to individual items. In (30) a high status person (who would normatively require honorification) gives something which the speaker considers undesirable, so that instead of the expected *kudasaru*, *kureru* is employed.

(30) a. The mayor *gives* me this rubbish.
      b. Shichōsan ga konna mono o *kureru*.

The elevating verb form expected (*kudasaru*) does not appear in (30) because of the negative aspect of what is being received. We realize from this that selectional specifications cannot be given for individual lexical items alone, as Harada and Prideaux suppose, but must refer to the entire semantic content of the sentence. It would be mistaken to believe that a restriction could be placed on *konna mono*, 'rubbish', such as [−Honorific] because, if whisky is given by the mayor instead of rubbish and 'I' turns out to be a teetotaller, disapproval could be similarly expressed using *kureru*. If 'I' were an alcoholic, *kudasaru* might well express appreciation of and respect for both the mayor and the drink. In such a case, a feature like [−Honorific] would be useless since whisky could take either and only the context (of the speaker's attitude) could determine which lexeme followed. In other words, well-formedness depends crucially on the summation of meaning in an utterance as well as on the circumstances surrounding the utterance (cf. Lakoff 1971: 333).

No semantic theory within generative grammar can handle this contextual relativity or deixis for such theories make no attempt to provide for any form-determining, extralinguistic factors. Katz and Fodor (1963: 179) justify their separation of linguistic knowledge from the rest of the knowledge a speaker has about the world by claiming that "there is no serious possibility of systematizing all the knowledge of the world that speakers have". But how can a semantic theory which does not admit the significance of social knowledge distinguish between *o-age ni naru* and *yaru?* Unfortunately, truth conditional semantics — the identification of meaning with the knowledge that makes meaning true or not — cannot serve us either. The verity of the sentence's meaning is not altered by whatever truth value a donatory form may hold. Allwood (1977: 153) sees no significance for truth conditional semantics arising from second person singular/plural distinctions in European languages:

> "if in a country like France, where there is a distinction between a formal and an informal second-person pronoun (*vous* and *tu*), one says after having invited some older person one does not know, 'tu es invité' (you are invited) this would be inappropriate but true".

If, however, a truth meaning such as 'the speaker does not show respect to the older person' is assigned to this utterance, it cannot be nullified nor altered in any way, such as by adding *mais je vous respecte* ('but I respect you') (cf. Levinson 1978: 7).

It should be evident by now that our data will not be explicated by a linguistic theory which fails to recognize the fact that the contents of an utterance does not solely depend on the isolated linguistic category of a sentence but also on a particular configuration of extralinguistic factors. If we are going to provide an adequate account of donatory forms it is impossible to bypass their deixis; we must construct a framework capable of handling a speaker's perception of his identity and the identity of those he is talking to and about.

A fruitful area to explore then is pragmatics which studies "linguistic acts and the contexts in which they are performed" (Stalnaker 1972: 383). Let us first turn to the pragmatic condition of presupposition which acknowledges a relation between a sentence and its users where X presupposes Y is the speaker, and in appropriately asserting X, has to believe Y to be true. Lakoff (1971) has convincingly demonstrated that sentences are well-formed only relative to the presuppositions on which they are based. Thus, sentence (31)b. is ill-formed because it does not accord with the "factual knowledge, cultural background, or beliefs about the world" (Lakoff 1971: 330):

(31) a. I *give* my friend a camera.
      b. Watashi ga tomodachi ni kamera o *o-age ni naru*.

One of the pragmatic presuppositions in (31) is[123] the speaker's assumption that his status warrants honorific reference to himself, a presupposition shared by no member of the Japanese speech community.

Such an argument may account for some of the data but before we begin an investigation we must remember that presuppositions are defeasible and honorifics, together with other socially deictic items, are not presuppositionally defeasible. There is no way of removing the presupposition in (31) that the speaker believes himself worthy of self-honorification. Moreover, the above presupposition cannot be blocked in an embedded clause cf. (32)b.

(32) a. He said, "I *give* my friend a camera".
      b. *Watashi ga tomadochi ni kamera o *o-age ni naru* to īmashita.

The plug "he said" does not cancel the presupposition that when he spoke about giving the camera, he presupposed his rank meritorious of honorific reference by himself.

Another potential candidate framework is that of Austin's speech acts (1962) — especially the category of illocutionary act, "an act done as conforming to a convention" (Austin 1975: 105) which belongs to all those "utterances which have a certain conventional force" (1975: 109). The illocutionary force of donatory verbs will be the respect or disrespect or equality that is made explicit by the particular selected form. On this view, the act of respecting or not respecting is conventionally encoded in what has been termed 'explicit performatives' such as "I order you to give me that"[124]. A formula such as "I order ... I promise, etc" serves to "make explicit and at the same time more precise what act it is that the speaker purports to perform in issuing his utterance" (Austin 1971: 16).

On this basis, we could interpret *kudasaru* in (33) as an explicit performative of respecting, which carries the illocutionary force roughly equivalent to "I respect the giver" — here the teacher.

(33) a. The teacher *gives* me a pen.
      b. Sensei ga pen o *kudasaru*.

Austin's felicity conditions (the rules determining the appropriateness of a performative utterance) seem particularly useful in blocking certain ill-formed utterances such as the application of the honorific for oneself in (31) by treating such occurrences as a breach of a conventional procedure resulting in a 'misfire'.

Morgan believes such conventions of usage to be a "matter of culture (manners, religion, law)" and "not knowledge of language per se" (1978: 269). However, once again the question must be reiterated: is there a neat dichotomy between cultural and linguistic knowledge?

It is only possible to use the illocutionary force indicating device for showing respect to a giver or receiver if the felicity conditions for such an act obtain (cf. Searle 1971: 49). The first of the felicity conditions that there "must exist an accepted conventional procedure having a certain conventional effect, the procedure to include the uttering of certain words by certain persons in certain circumstances" (Austin 1975: 26) could capture some of the constraints on donatory forms (i.e. the conventional procedure is to acknowledge the social position of certain givers and receivers with a particular form. For reasons to be discussed shortly, we do not consider this to be the most satisfactory framework for handling such constraints, principally because Austin's account provides no foundation for evaluating interpersonal relations — which, of course, it never set out to do.

However, a considerable amount of work on honorifics has been carried out on the basis of the abstract-performative hypothesis, as developed by Ross (1968) and (1970), McCawley (1970) and Lewis (1972). Such analyses consider every sentence to have as its highest deep syntactic and semantic clause a structure like those that give rise to explicit performatives[125]. Sadock (1974: 42-43) argues for the treatment of particularly addressee but also referent honorifics within this framework. Instead of a special politeness morpheme as discussed above (such as the SSS feature), Noun Phrases referring to the speaker and addressee shoud bear status markers, it is suggested.

Makino's performative account deals solely with addressee honorifics and not referent honorifics which we are dealing with here but it is interesting to quote the problem he encountered in applying politeness trar.sformations: he found that the grammar could not "mechanically identify the relative height of two human nouns" (1970: 179), cf. sentences (27) and (28). Makino's inability to "build an account of relative social hierarchy into the deep structure" (1970: 179) is apparently overcome in Hinds' (1976) modifications of Ross' proposals whereby the former forcibly demonstrates the need for a context-orientated analysis of Japanese because only such an analysis "allows a more general statement to be made concerning the acceptability/unacceptability of certain types of constructions" (Hinds 1976: 113); he also argues for a performative analysis since it is capable of dealing with the "considerable degree of difference between language used by Japanese males and Japanese females, particularly in terms of particle usage and lexical selection". Of course, these remarks are very important when one remembers the sex-biased restrictions on *yaru*.

From Hinds' examples (1976b: 114-115) the following abstract tree structure has been drawn showing a male saying that he gives a pen to his friend:

(35)

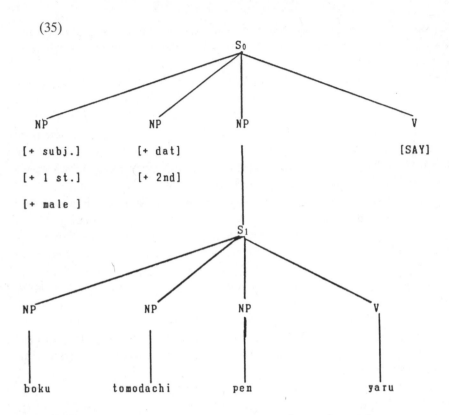

Hinds' proposed features are very extensive as he wishes to cover a whole sociolinguistic range of data such as [+ old]. [Kagoshima dialect], [± child], [± adult] and account for differences that occur in elderly and regional speech as well as the way adults address children. Hinds points out that addressee and referent honorifics are closely connected and apply to a notion of formality and therefore introduces this as a feature. To represent the hierarchy of interpersonal relations, he uses an integer taken from a scale of one through ten where the number ten represents the highest level in the social scale and one the lowest. Hinds sees five as neutral and therefore chooses it to designate the speaker. These integers are attached to the speaker node, addressee node and nodes extending from any relevant subject or object nodes in the sentence itself.

Again working on the basis of Hinds' examples (1976b: 134-138) we can show in (36) how such an analysis is capable of dealing with an utterance reflecting the various social relations that hold between a speaker addressing his section chief at work about the department chief's (kachō) act of giving. We do not show the tree for the actual sentence uttered, but presume that an interpretive rule would select an honorific form in this case such as *o-age ni naru*.

With this framework we could never generate any unacceptable utterances such as (26)b. where a younger brother was honorificated by the speaker since here a younger brother would be represented with a lower scaling than the speaker (such as 4) as either subject of object in the lower sentence (S1). Of course, a feature such as [± ingroup] will be necessary to distinguish between *kudasaru* and *ageru* but this should not be problematic, as long as there is a rule which states that *kureru/kudasaru* may be selected on condition that the subject i.e. the giver in S1 is not an ingroup member at the same time as the object in S1 is a group member.

Clearly, such an analysis should be able to deal effectively with the generation of donatory forms of any variety, including those which refer to

(36)

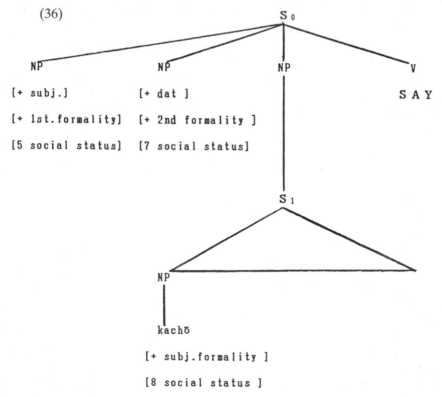

absolute statuses cf. the opening section of this paper, as well as those with a socially deictic content. However, problems with the performative analysis are numerous (cf. Cohen 1970, Fraser 1971, Wunderlich 1971: 170 and Grewendorf 1972: 144-182), although Hinds' modified framework seems to overcome some of these shortcomings: overt reference to 'I' or 'you' is not considered essential; anaphoric phenomena are handled by being entered in a temporary section of a special component called the registry, defined as "an adjunct store of information used to record concepts" (1976b: 26).

Of course, the paradox of the performative approach (Braunroth 1975: 48) is the fact that in order to account for pragmatic or contextual constraints linguists opted for a theoretical construct (TG) to build on which was originally developed to handle the purely formal aspects of a sentence with complete disregard for the indexicality of sentences or their elements. The inability of such a framework to handle so-called nonstandard language (cf. Wunderlich 1971: 176, and Grewendorf 1972: 168-169) when, for example, an honorific is used to express discontent or gratitude and its 'meaning' cannot be reduced to the mere expression of respect, as well as its inability to cope with deictic phenomena whether local, temporal or interpersonal, have led some linguists to adopt a different approach entirely.

For instance, Brown and Levinson (1978) consider social deixis to be unaccountable either within traditional semantics or performative theories. Instead, communication is viewed as working on rational lines and deference interpreted as the addressee's "want to have his freedom of action unhindered and his attention unimpeded" (1978: 134).

Following this view, variation in donatory forms corresponds to a variation in communicative strategies or ways in interacting to obtain particular rational goals. Thus, Levinson considers socially deictic items best handled by the Gricean notion of "conventional implicature" which includes all "non truth-conditional aspects of what is conveyed by an utterance solely due to the words or forms the sentence contains" (Sadock 1978: 282). In the sentence "He is an Englishman; he is therefore, brave" 'therefore' *conventionally implicates* that "it follows from his being an Englishman that he is brave" (Grice 1975: 45). The advantage over presuppositions is that conventional implicatures "just can't be blocked" (Sadock 1978: 293). The implicature made above is not cancelled in the negative (he is not an Englishman; he is, therefore, not brave) and cannot be related to any truth conditions (the link between "he is an Englishman" and he is "brave" is not necessarily true). So conventional implicatures appear to provide the long sought correspondence between context and linguistic form.

Scales of implicated deference are created by Levinson (1977: 36) to account for honorifics together with other socially deictic items where a horizontal axis indicates social distance from the speaker and a vertical axis indicates superiority and higher social status. If the honorifics are symmetrically exchanged, then the horizontal axis of social distance is implicated. If they are exchanged assymetrically then, the scale of power is implicated. A number scale is also provided to "represent the degree to which the addressee is socially distant from the speaker ... the other (number scale) will represent the degree to which the addressee has a higher social status than the addressed" (Levinson 1977: 37).

These deference scales provide us simultaneously with an honorifics generating device and a meaning indicating device, as shown below. If the plotting of the donatory forms is correct, it is obvious that some forms such as *kudasaru* will have to be considered as containing two conventional implicatures: firstly, that the receiver belongs closely to the speaker's group and secondly, that the giver was either socially more distant or more superior and of higher social status than the receiver.

Ingroup belongingness must be considered a conventional implicature, otherwise, as well as there being no way to differentiate between *kudasaru* and *sashiageru*, there would be no explanation for not assigning honorifics to younger brother i.e. ingroup members who are inferior to the speaker, as well as other family members when addressing outsiders, and no explanation for the blocking of an honorific usage where it occurred with an ingroup member as in (16)b.

In order to work out the conventional implicatures of donatory forms, the speaker is placed at the centre of the two axes (3). If the recipient is superior to the speaker e.g. at 5, the latter receives *sashiageru*. If he is inferior to the speaker on the social status axis, then *yaru*. If very distant on the social distance axis, then *sashiageru* or *o-age itasu/suru*; if equal to the speaker, then *ageru* (cf. Brown and Gilman's two dimensional semantic for T/V pronouns, 1972: 259). Although this framework deals adequately with the "bulk of socially deictic items in Tamil" (Levinson 1977: 38), it is not adequate enough for sentences such as (37).

    (37)   a. I give you a camera (where you = my father)
            b. Watashi ga kamera o *ageru*[126].

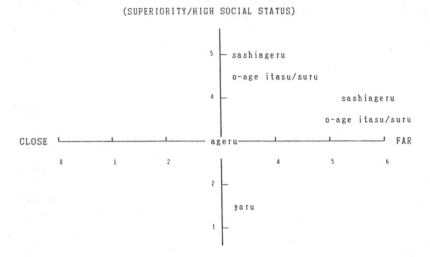

Diagram 4. Scales of implicational deference where the giver is the speaker

If one looks at the scales of implicated deference as represented in Diagram 4, *ageru* carries the conventional implicature of equal social status between donor and recipient where the two axes converge at 3. The dimension of 'intimacy' does not get encoded in donatory verbs. Ogasawara (1972: 26) claims that the Western politeness axis is horizontal and based on intimacy versus formality while the Japanese axis is vertical and based on status/ age inferiority versus superiority. Also it should be noted that *ageru* has been centrally placed so as to indicate giving to those 'close'.

What are the consequences of the above for (37)b? The implicature of social symmetry (from *ageru*) does not correspond at all to the 'conventional' Japanese view of a father-son relationship where the household head is supposed to command much authority[127]. If the implicature here is that the speaker and his father are socially equal or intimate, this is clearly misleading and false[128]. It should be added, that this is the standard way of referring to giving something to one's father. *Sashiageru* or *o-age suru* would generally be considered inappropriate[129] and *yaru* would imply a father's inferior status, constituting an insult in this context.

Similarly, conventional implicature seems unable to cope with instances of a high status person receiving no honorific:

(38) a. Kodomo ga *shichōsan* to chichi ni hana o *ageru*.
b. The child *gives* the *mayor* and my father some flowers.

As *ageru* would conventionally implicate equality between givers and receivers and this is obviously not the case in (38) where a child is giving socially upwards to a high-ranking official, *shichōsan* and where it would be normally appropriate to have selected *sashiageru*, the implicature has obviously been cancelled. Now Sadock (1978: 292) has stated that a key property of conventional implicatures is that they "can be called into question without producing infelicity, but none can be denied". Yet in both (37) and (38) this is precisely what has happened. Wilson's claim (1975: 116) that if conventional implicatures appear to be cancelled, they are "not really ... at all but merely interpreted as coming from someone other than the speaker" offers no way out since *watashi*, 'I', can be none other than the speaker and *chichi* is the lexeme for 'my father' — anybodyelse's would have to be *otōsan*.

The issue at stake here directly relates to the dilemma of separating meaning from use, a fundamental problem which bears on the distinction between form and function, competence and performance, linguistic system and socio-cultural framework. Fodor (1977: 19) writes on Wittgenstein lines that:

> "it is a serious as well as silly mistake to regard meanings as ENTITIES that stand in some special relation to expressions ... Language is integrated into our behaviour and our interactions with others in an intimate way ... Language should be viewed not as an abstract calculus but as a tool, and just like a hammer or a can opener, the proper characterization of a linguistic expression must include an account of how it is used and what it is used for".

Is it all possible to assign one basic abstract meaning to an honorific? Surely, use cannot be explained in terms of meaning alone nor vice versa. It is true that sometimes donatory forms such as *sashiageru* etc. conventionally implicate 'social distance' or 'superiority' but at other times meaning is to be derived from their contexts of occurrence. The 'meaning' of contemporary Japanese honorifics should not be reduced to the mere expression of social relationships. Honorifics in Japanese are, in fact, frequently used to indicate fictive statuses (cf. ch.1., section 1.2.1.). The meaning of an honorific form cannot be solely identical with one particular interpretation but is context-dependent.

In order to semantically differentiate between Japanese donatory verbs, we are forced to look at their contexts of use since the former all contain the basic notion of *giving*. Furthermore, as we have seen in sentences (13), (14), (24) and (26), what constitutes a grammatically acceptable sentence is frequently socioculturally determined.

Apart from this difficulty, the crucial question of whose grammar the linguist chooses to formalize has already been raised above in connection with Harada's (1975: 547) acknowledgement of the variation between Japanese speakers in their honorific usage. The validity of a description of ideal competence becomes doubtful when Neustupný (1978: 237), for instance, specifically states that his account of honorifics "is based on the contemporary variety used in conversation by middle-aged university educated speakers from the Tokyo area" which is, in fact, the general model for most Japanese honorific accounts. However, selection of any social group for linguistic idealization is hardly justifiable on a scientific basis.

By now it should be patently clear that we must have a context- and speaker-differentiating, socioculturally sensitive analysis capable of dealing with interactants' relationships and intentions. As yet no such linguistic framework exists. Clearly, it cannot derive from the realms of traditional syntax nor semantics, since these have maintained the structuralist rejection of all pertaining to the extralinguistic. Neither can the answer lie in the mere welding of a communication-oriented, logico-philosophical analysis onto an essentially structuralist base as has been the case within certain areas of pragmatics.

If linguistic theory is going to achieve its goal of satisfactorily describing and explaining *langue*, it must now turn to that 'messy' reality it has up till now restrained itself from utilizing, namely *parole* and develop a socio-psychologically based grammar. The latter should not be conceived in purely functional terms nor simply classificatory in terms of variation and variety. Instead various theoretical strands must be woven into a new integrative description which takes into account the inextricable interconnections between individual and linguistic system.

4.   CROSS-CULTURAL CONTRASTS

This final chapter focusses on contrasts in linguistic behaviour between Japanese and English communities. It may also be considered as relevant to the general discussion of differences between Japan and the West. The first section presents a novel sociolinguistic approach in phonetic research and deals specifically with the pitch correlates of politeness. The results of the study show that Japanese female subjects adopt an extremely high pitch separating themselves acoustically from Japanese males in the same circumstances, while English male pitch demonstrates much less differentiation from English female pitch. The social significance of these findings is then examined.

The last section surveys and classifies areas of mutual misunderstanding in diverse areas of Japanese-Western communication under the concept of 'semiotic schism'. It looks at interaction as symbolic and interprets it from a social psychological perspective. Its ultimate aim is to analyse the process of cross-cultural conflict and suggest ways to avoid it.

4.1. Pitch, politeness and sexual role

This investigation ventures to demonstrate how intonational differences occurring in the expression of politeness[130] in English and Japanese can be related to the two language communities' sociocultural expectations of and attitudes towards male and female pitch. The inspiration for the study arose from the comments of a Japanese who remarked how 'feminine' he felt when using polite English intonation.

Like most suprasegmental properties of speech, pitch and its related features like intonation have traditionally been considered as belonging on the periphery of the linguistic system and until recently, particularly with the development of the technical means for their analysis, pitch phenomena have not received the attention they deserve.

However, increasingly, the multifunctional contribution of pitch and its related features to the generation (Chomsky and Halle 1968) and interpretation of language has been recognized. Out of the mass of research conducted on prosodic features in recent times, it is the grammatical aspects of pitch that emerge as the main focus of research, while the semantic (attitudinal and emotional) correlates of pitch have been the subject of only occasional study; needless to say, the sociocultural correlates of pitch have hardly received any treatment at all.

4.1.1. *Pitch*

Although it is a mistake to regard pitch solely as a function of fundamental frequency because other factors such as the level of intensity at which judgements are made, the type of person and the physical parameters involved (cf. Crystal 1969: 109), the length of the sound presented for analysis and the segmental quality of the utterance[131] also affect pitch perception, the principal correlate of the pitch of complex tones is the fundamental frequency of the periodic sound which does correspond to the frequency of the vibration of the vocal cords (Fry 1968: 374 and Ladefoged 1975: 162) and, for the purposes of this study, it is assumed that the instrumental measurement of fundamental frequency is related to the psychobiological perception of pitch.

According to Crystal (1975: 94), there are two systems of pitch: one is *tone* which refers to "the direction of pitch movement in a syllable, as when it falls, rises, or stays level, or does some of these things in rapid succession", and the other is *pitch range* i.e.

> "the distance between adjacent syllables or stretches of utterance identified in terms of a scale running from low to high. Speakers and groups have a normal pitch-level and range, and they may depart from this in different ways to produce extra-high or low speech, either in a sudden step-up or down, or gradually. The normal distance between adjacent syllables may be narrowed (perhaps reduced to monotone) or widened, and different languages display different kinds and degrees of pitch-variation. The patterns of pitch-movement that occur in a language are referred to as the *intonation*".

This investigation concentrates on this second aspect of pitch — *pitch range* — and tries to compare the normal pitch-level of the two language groups while expressing the same semantic content. In this connection, it is worth noting the comments of Edelsky (1979: 28) who, failing to correlate sex with specific intonation patterns in an empirical study, writes that "... the actual production of particular direction alone in terminal contours ... is probably not one of" the factors to be considered in sex-differentiated language research. However, Edelsky believes that other "intonational variables such as ... *peak pitch*, *pitch* at the turning point preceding the terminal glide ... and others already identified as sex-linked, such as overall pitch,

pitch variability ... might be more profitable areas of pursuit if one is trying to find production differences" (my emphasis).

Of course, variations in pitch-levels (intonation) do not occur in isolation but are accompanied in speech by a very complex set of other acoustic features — some prosodic such as loudness, rhythmicality and tempo in particular (Crystal 1975: 11) and others such as voice quality (Laver 1975). Unfortunately, none of these important accompanying features can be considered here due to limitations of research. Before an account of the investigation is given, it might be useful to very briefly examine the principal characteristics of and contrasts between the Japanese and English intonation systems.

4.1.1.1. *Japanese use of pitch*

There has been a great amount of research on Japanese pitch accent (cf. National Language Research Institute 1951 and Martin 1967) but information on further aspects of Japanese intonation is very scanty indeed. Every Japanese word has an inherent accent pattern which may be occasionally phonemic but is not necessarily so. This accent patterning varies according to dialect regions and also according to speaker age. A description of the Japanese pitch-accent is complicated by the superimposition of pitch changes carrying syntactic and attitudinal functions onto the accent patterns. However, Abe (1955: 338) maintains that the overlapping of pitch accent patterns with intonation in Japanese does not seem to significantly alter the basic tonal structure of a word. It would seem that the final particles in Japanese e.g. *yo*, *ne*, *zo*, *wa*[132] serve as significant indicators of emotional state (cf. Wenk 1954: 120-121 and Martin 1954: 27). It should be added here that no reference in the literature could be found concerning the socioculturally determined differences in Japanese male and female intonation constituting the field of this study.

4.1.1.2. *English use of pitch (British)*

A review of research and theory relating to English intonation is obviously beyond the scope of this section; in fact, Crystal (1969) provides an exhaustive survey of English prosodic studies. As mentioned before, pitch does not occur in isolation but is accompanied by many other interrelated features that are fundamental to any description of the English prosodic system. Problems in the analysis of English intonation have arisen because of the difficulties in drawing a clear boundary line between the effect of pitch contrast and the above mentioned accompanying suprasegmental features. Generally, intonational research has lacked valid empirical support and neglected the semantic and social aspects of intonation mainly because of the difficulties arising from technical analysis. Furthermore, where frameworks have been set up such as by Pike (1945) or O'Connor and Arnold (1973) according to Crystal (1969: 290) there has been oversimplification, imprecision and impressionism.

In spite of the multiplicity of features involved in English intonation, one fact stands out in all the research: "... the most readily perceivable, recurrent, maximal functional unit to which linguistic meanings can be attached (in the present state of our knowledge) is the tone unit" (Crystal 1969: 204). It is on this basis that O'Connor and Arnold (1973) analyze the structure of English intonation in terms of a nuclear tone and optional additions such as tail, head, or pre-head[133]. For O'Connor and Arnold (1973) it is the contrasts in falls and rises between three pitch levels (high, mid and low) that signal grammatical meaning such as statements, questions, commands and exclamations as well as attitudinal/emotional meaning which they label with adjectives such as 'detached', 'surly', 'astonished', 'concerned', 'hurt' etc. Crystal (1969: 201) also stresses the fact that "it has long been realised that, within the prosodic contrasts in English, some features are more noticeable and seem to carry more semantic 'weight' than others"; these salient features to which Crystal is referring are those primarily connected with pitch and stress. At the present time, however, there is no developed semantic theory of intonation nor an explanation of how it cofunctions with syntax, nor any detailed study of its sociolinguistic correlates, i.e. sex, group membership, situation and so forth.

4.1.2. *Interference*

This is a term from behaviourist psychology which is taken here to signify the negative effect of borrowing a feature from one's first language in expressing oneself in a second, thereby violating a norm of the second language. Because of the variations between the two language communities' prosodic systems sketched out above, it is to be assumed that Japanese non-native speakers of English may produce suprasegmental interference, especially when expressing emotion (cf. Pürschel 1975: 17)

Strangely enough, Abe (1955) and Shimaoka (1966) do not mention differences in pitch level at all between English and Japanese in their contrastive research. Shimaoka (1966: 358) maintains that, as pitch variation has a phonemic function in Japanese, the rise and falls of English intonation should not be too difficult a problem, even though Japanese speakers have great difficulty in controlling the rise and fall because the transitions between pitch levels by Japanese speakers were found to be much more "abrupt" than the smooth transitions of the American subjects. These findings are supported by the study, but Shimaoka's hypothesis that Japanese speakers are all well able to imitate English rises is especially challenged.

Abe's investigation of English and Japanese intonation brought him to the conclusion that "the psychological channelling of voice in English and Japanese seems to have much in common, particularly with reference to such crucial tunes as in questions and statements" (Abe 1955: 346). However, it is the purpose of this study to show that the channelling of pitch-level in English and Japanese is essentially different principally for the male speakers of the two languages.

4.1.3. *The investigation*

The method of obtaining data was as follows. Altogether ten informants were selected, five from each language group and for each group there were two females and three males. Unfortunately, the subjects' ages were not all similar, and the possible consequences of this will shortly be discussed. The two female Japanese speakers were 28 and 29 and the two British English female speakers 23 and 25. The Japanese male subjects were 36, 42 and 44, while the British male speakers were 24, 39 and 46 (cf. also section 4.1.3.1. below).

The subjects were asked to read a certain role in a short written dialogue[134] of an emotionally neutral character. The dialogue contained politeness formulae, such as the greetings 'oh hello' (*ā konnichi wa*) and 'bye' (*sayonara*), with a 'thank you' (*arigato gozaimasu*) in the middle of the text. These three formulae from the core of the comparisons and were edited out and subjected to technical measurement.

The Japanese subjects were asked to read a certain role (A) in the freely translated Japanese text as well as in the English version. The same role (A) was taken by the English subjects. All those involved were told that they should attempt as natural speech as possible; the dangers inherent in this kind of recording are discussed in section 4.1.3.1. below. The subjects were also asked to imagine that they were meeting B in the street and that the latter was a non-intimate acquaintance whom they had not seen for some time. The investigator assumed the role of B throughout — in both Japanese and English, hoping thereby to keep one variable constant.

The decision to use pre-written material was adopted for various reasons. Firstly, there was the impossibility of capturing informants' natural conversation in which utterances of a truly comparable character, i.e. where a similar physical, psychological and social setting could be guaranteed (cf. Edelsky 1979). Secondly, the technical unreliability of natural recordings is infamous.

When the subjects had been recorded, their data were analysed on a pitch meter, an instrument giving a time frequency display of the F_0 of the voice, and, in order to verify the validity of these findings, spectrograms of the politeness formulae in both languages were made on the sound spectrograph. Furthermoore, the Low distortion oscillator was employed to establish the subjects' phonational ranges by matching the subjects' pitch level by ear[135] to the frequency output of the oscillator.

4.1.3.1. *Variables*

There are five typical variables involved in any analysis of pitch and intonation:

(i) The physical and temporal circumstances of the study. By this is meant the complex of situational features in which informants are recorded[136]. As stated earlier, the recordings were made inside a sound-proof studio with a microphone dangling obtrusively in front of the informant's face. Of course, this is not similar to any natural face-to-face encounter, and the investigator is well aware that the artificiality of the situation could have provoked an unnatural performance on the subject's part. Moreover, Cooper and Yanagihara (1971) discovered that basal pitch level, the lowest note on which an utterance can be sustained, does not remain stable throughout the day but varies according to the time, either continually rising or falling throughout the day with a "pitch rise at noon followed by a lowering of pitch in the late afternoon" (1971: 265). However these findings are not taken into account here and must be regarded as a further variable.

(ii) Another important factor relates to the "emotional state" of the subjects recorded. Deva's (1957, 1958, 1960) long-term study of Telugu intonation indicated that "pitch level and range are significant differentia of emotions. No inflectional characteristics are of any importance at this level" (Deva 1960: 27) and it is to be expected that a subject's psychological condition at the time of recording, i.e. if he/she is nervous, relaxed, depressed, elated etc. will influence the performance considerably.

(iii) Another essential variable is the nature of the social relationship holding between the subject and the person with whom he/she interacts during the recording. It can generally be said that the relationship towards the investigator was one of causal acquaintance for all but one of the informants. However, all subjects were requested to simulate the surprise meeting of two rather distant acquaintances. Also bearing on the nature of the interactions is the social variety of language employed in the study. It is hoped that the essentially remote social relationship shared by the speakers (A and B) is reflected in the fairly formal dialogue.

(iv) An uncontrollable variable is that of individual differences between the subjects. The variation in age has already been mentioned above; anatomical changes resulting from ageing, such as the lowering of the larynx and atrophy of muscles and disturbance of the mucus supply (Laber 1975: 364) which affect voice quality and, in turn, pitch level, do not occur until senility and are thus irrelevant here, although the subjects' age variation must be a significant variable. Other idiosyncratic differences include the level of English proficiency attained by the Japanese informants. How competent in English prosodics were they? All Japanese subjects had learnt English in Japan as part of formal education and claimed to have received little if no training in the suprasegmental sphere. An attempt to eliminate regional and social variation in the English speakers was made by the investigator's selection of informants considered to be speakers of Received Pronunciation, traditionally viewed as the standard variety of oral British (English) English. All the English informants are university educated as are the Japanese speakers; they were subjectively judged to be capable of speaking an educated and essentially standard variety of their native language. Furthermore, the Japanese speakers are roughly divided between the major dialect regions of Japan: from western Japan one male (Kyoto) and one female (Takamatsu) while from eastern Japan two males (Tokyo) and one female (Tokyo).

(v) It is obvious that the analysis of reading voices is problematic if generalizations concerning the natural use of language are being made. How valid an indicator of a subject's pitch use in natural contexts is the recording of his/her reading a role? There cannot, of course, be anything beyond a postulated correspondence between the two. Factors, such as an awareness of how one usually interacts with one's pitch and an ability to consciously reproduce it, may be important.

4.1.3.2. *Results*

In spite of the set of uncontrollable variables outlined above inherent in any analysis of pitch, it is remarkable that on inspection of the data there is such a close correspondence between the various groups of speakers' performances.

Before any comparative statement about the subjects' pitch levels can be made, however, it is important to establish their phonational ranges.

Table 4 shows the phonational ranges of the subjects which were measured with the aid of a low distortion oscillator.

From now on, the subjects will be referred to as Japanese Male (JM), English Male (EM), Japanese Female (JF) and English Female (EF). They will also be assigned a number by which they will always be designated.

Table 4. *The phonational ranges of the subjects*

SUBJECTS & AGES	LOWEST FREQUENCY	HIGHEST FREQUENCY
JM_1 (36)	75 Hz	360 Hz
JM_2 (42)	68 Hz	355 Hz
JM_3 (44)	75 Hz	390 Hz
JF_1 (28)	120 Hz	1,050 Hz
JF_2 (29)	110 Hz	620 Hz
—————	—————	—————
EM_1 (24)	78 Hz	380 Hz
EM_2 (39)	75 Hz	380 Hz
EM_3 (46)	70 Hz	390 Hz
EF_1 (23)	110 Hz	990 Hz
EF_2 (25)	120 Hz	550 Hz

Hollien, Dew and Philips (1971: 755) found the mean values for the lowest and highest frequencies of phonation for American males to be 78 and 698 Hz respectively, while the lowest and highest frequencies for American females were 139 and 1,108 Hz respectively. The phonational ranges presented here do not seriously conflict with these findings. Denes (1959) and Denes and Milton-Williams (1962) measured frequencies for a representative group of British speakers and established ranges of 66-411 Hz for male speakers and 75-508 Hz for females. Although these findings correspond to the English males in this study, Denes' very low female range was not captured by means of the low pitch oscillator but *is revealed* in the performance of the English female subjects described below. It is worth noting Fry's observation (1968: 389) that "the fundamental frequencies occurring in speech have been measured by various workers and the range and mean values have been *variously* estimated" (my emphasis). Finally, in connection with the phonational ranges presented in Table 4, the disparity caused by JF_1 should be explained; she is a soprano singer.

Before discussing the frequency measurements of the politeness formulae, the question of tonal relativity must be raised. As Abercrombie (1967: 107) stresses, it is the position of the points on a frequency scale relative to each other that counts in an analysis of intonation. It is not the frequency in terms of number of vibrations per second that is significant but the intervals between these points which are always relative and variable in the patterns of speech melody. However, this study does not postulate any ideal tones for 'polite' melodies in either language community but simply aims at contrasting the overall pitch level of polite utterances in English and Japanese on the basis of speaker's sex.

Although no absolute statements regarding pitch level can be made, it is generally recognized that "the number of discriminations possible at any given reference level is extremely restricted" (Crystal 1975: 77). Furthermore, it seems that we do not hear unlimited variability between individuals. "Speakers learn a finite set of standardized perceptual values, derived from a selection of the available range of vocal effects (including pitch) which combine in various ways to produce a set of semantic stereotypes" (Crystal 1975: 80). Relating to and supporting this view[137], it is plain from both Tables 2 and 3, indicating the beginning and end F_0 and the peak and end F_0, that native speakers do appear to be aiming at a certain *pitch band* and are always within an average narrow band of 100 Hz. Similarly, the Japanese males' pitch level coincides remarkably, as does the female Japanese pitch. This would substantiate the claim that pitch norms exist and may be definable in terms of F_0 (cf. Crystal 1975: 80-82). Also related to this matter are the comments of Luchsinger and Arnold (1965: 100) about a central pitch level (the average speaking level) around which prosodic inflection is closely concentrated. They locate this average speaking level at the "lower border of the physiological vocal range".

Although research has shown that certain vowels and consonants have an inherently higher frequency than others, e.g. [i], [u] and [s], such segmental differences are not relevant here, as we are comparing identical segments and considering whole units.

Moreover, we have not examined the first prominent syllable of a tone unit which, according to Crystal (1975: 81) provides "the most consistent approximation to a pitch level towards which a speaker automatically tends to return for the commencement of a new tone unit", primarily because our focus is on the tonal expression of politeness formulae in the two language communities and not necessarily on the speaking level for normal, continual conversation, since, as the results presented below illustrate, there exist interesting pitch differences in the way English and Japanese speakers express politeness.

Some of the results obtained by means of the pitch meter are clearly incorrect, particularly those measurements of very low and very high pitch (this fact was revealed when the same utterances were subjected to spectrographic analysis). The frequent reading of 70 Hz for the Japanese men is most improbable, considering that this represents the absolute minimum of the male phonational range; see Hollien, Dew and Philips (1971: 75) who found 78 Hz as the lowest mean phonational frequency in their investigations. However, this does not alter the fact that the pitch level of the Japanese males was generally lower than that of the English males and this is also reflected in frequency readings obtained from spectograms.

It must be remembered when comparing the results obtained from the two instruments (pitch meter and spectrograph) that the pitch meter gives an overall average frequency for an utterance visually represented in the form of a horizontal line while the spectrograph offers a temporally more detailed picture, allowing for the frequency measurement at a particular point during the utterance, and that is why the peak of the utterance is taken as a unit of spectrographic measurement and the beginning of the utterance for pitch meter analysis. These two measurements are completely distinct and are not intended for direct comparison. However, there should, of course, be some

Table 5. The fundamental frequency in Hz of Japanese and English politeness formulae obtained by pitch meter at the beginning and end of each utterance.

SUBJECTS	BEGINNING ā konnichi wa	END	BEGINNING arigatō gozaimasu	END	BEGINNING sayonara	END
JM₁	50	70	90	90	90	90
JM₂	70	60	80	80	70	70
JM₃	70	75	90	80	70	70
JF₁	250	185	250	220	250	200
JF₂	250	180	300	250	250	250
	oh hello		thankyou		bye	
EM₁	200	185	200	180	200	200
EM₂	250	200	200	100	120	100
EM₃	250	200	185	60	100	70
EF₁	250	170	250	170	220	200
EF₂	250	250	250	100	110	100
JM₁	70	90	70	60	70	80
JM₂	70	80	80	70	70	60
JM₃	170	115	200	90	80	70
JF₁	250	325	160	120	250	180
JF₂	300	340	280	140	250	250

Table 6. The fundamental frequency in Hz of Japanese and English politeness formulae obtained by spectrographic analysis at the peak and end of each utterance.

SUBJECTS	PEAK ā konnichi wa	END	PEAK arigatō gozaimasu	END	PEAK sayonara	END
JM₁	100	90	100	85	120	90
JM₂	90	85	90	80	100	80
JM₃	110	90	95	80	100	90
JF₁	400	200	450	380	390	350
JF₂	400	190	310	290	310	270
	oh hello		thankyou		bye	
EM₁	190	95	310	140	190	180
EM₂	250	100	200	90	170	100
EM₃	120	200	190	70	100	90
EF₁	270	260	320	150	220	190
EF₂	300	150	230	110	160	120
JM₁	100	95	90	85	85	85
JM₂	90	100	95	90	90	80
JM₃	200	190	200	100	100	90
JF₁	310	130	400	260	220	160
JF₂	300	160	380	110	300	250

degree of correlation between the subjects' frequency as recorded on the pitch meter and the peak frequency of the same utterance as analysed by the spectrograph i.e. the relative variation in the subjects' performance should remain constant.

Finally, it is clear from comparing the frequency findings of both instruments that the pitch meter tends to indicate values that are too low for tones.

4.1.4. *Interpretation of the results*

The subjects' phonational ranges do not seem so divergent as to nullify the study. In fact, they correspond surprisingly closely. In spite of the fact that Japanese male phonational limits are 68, 75 and 75 Hz and the English male phonational limits are 70, 75 and 78 Hz. Japanese males consistently adopt a much lower level of pitch in Japanese (80-120 Hz according to the spectrographic findings) than do their English counterparts whose range lies between 70 and 310 Hz. All three English males produced a tone of 190 Hz, while only one Japanese male speaker (JM1) hit 120 Hz saying *sayonara*. One Japanese speaker (JM2) never reached a frequency beyond 100 Hz in expressing any of the politeness formulae. Two out of the three Japanese male subjects seemed to transfer their low pitch level (by English norms) into their English performance. Only one (JM3) was aware of higher pitch 'norms' and attempted to aim for these, although never surpassing the English males, as his top frequency in English was 300 Hz. It must be added, however, that this speaker's (JM3) English pitch contours sounded unnatural with high nuclear tones occurring apparently at random. From this it is clear that even though all male speakers from both linguistic groups share an almost identical phonational minimum, the Japanese males have restricted themselves here to a frequency maximum of about 120 Hz which English males do not hesitate to exceed. What is interesting, therefore, is that the Japanese males' preferred top pitch is much lower than the English males', in spite of the fact that both groups of males have a broadly similar phonational range. Furthermore, the English males' performance certainly reaches and sometimes equals the English females' top range, while this is never the case with Japanese males in relation to Japanese females.

The Japanese female subjects adopt an extremely high pitch in expressing Japanese politeness formulae, clearly separating themselves from Japanese males. This sharp pitch distinction between the sexes is not reproduced so obviously in the perpermance of the English subjects. English female pitch is considerably less differentiated from English male pitch. It was evident on listening to the Japanese females' production of politeness formulae that they were adopting an 'artificially' high F_0 level such as 450 Hz. The frequency band separating the Japanese males from Japanese females in the Japanese utterance is between 100 and 150 Hz on both spectrographic and pitch meter readings. In contrast, the English male and female subjects are only separated within a comparatively extremely narrow band of 20-50 Hz.

Japanese females seem to lower their 'high' pitch slightly at the ends of utterances in English, and this generally coincides within the native speaker frequency range but sometimes lies above it. Similarly, Japanese males transfer their comparatively low pitch to English, with the exception of JM_3 mentioned above.

These findings suggest that there are very clear sex-based intonational differences in the expression of politeness formulae for Japanese speakers that do not hold for English speakers with similar lower phonational limits. The pitch level of the Japanese subjects in the study demonstrably separates the sexes, while the boundaries of pitch are less sexually marked for English speakers.

4.1.4.1. *Semantic implications*

As O'Connor and Arnold (1973: 5) state, "every utterance we make contains in its intonation, some indication of ... (an) attitude ... The English speaker learns by experience from earliest childhood what attitudes are linked with the various tunes he hears and uses, but he would be hard put to it to explain them". Many very complex problems are involved in the semantic labelling of tonal variations. One of the reasons for not presenting to native speaker judges the performance of the Japanese subjects in English was the difficulty in erasing the accompanying segmental features and voice quality. There is no fully developed theory at the present time explaining the delicate relationship between attitudinal and emotional meaning and pitch, but research has indicated that certain "contrasts enter into the definition of many labels and have an extremely important attitudinal role to play" (Crystal 1969: 306) such as falling tone, large step-up in pitch, low pitch, high pitch range, rising-falling tone, step-downs, wide and narrow pitch-range, for example.

Accordingly, it is to be expected that the low pitch performance of Japanese male speakers in English will be semantically significant. Pike (1945: 59) claims that politeness/cheerfulness may be emphasized by stepping up pitch and, most interestingly, states that this higher step-up suggests "lightness" and "femininity". Level contours carry connotations of "ruggedness". These comments are reflected in the findings: all English speakers raised their pitch considerably when thanking B for an invitation to dinner. The two Japanese male speakers did not, and this may be unfavourably interpreted in English, as various studies indicate that flat, low tones (and this is what the Japanese male subjects invariably produced) imply "absence of emotional involvement", "routineness", "unsociability", "being cool, irritated, rude" (Crystal 1975: 38-9) as well as "bored", "angry, matter-of-fact, vexed, impatient, satisfied, grim" (Crystal 1969: 305). Uldall (1964) found that a narrow pitch range had definitely "unpleasant" associations for those judging it. Moreover, Leed (1965: 59) notes the negative reaction of Americans to the "low level pitch" of Russian speakers of English.

4.1.4.2. *Sociocultural implications*

In the above section, the possible differences in the way the two language communities process pitch correlates of politeness have been sketched out. It does not appear to be considered 'rude' for Japanese males to express politeness in Japanese within a narrow pitch range.

In relation to culturally varying interpretations of pitch use, Luchsinger and Arnold (1965: 100) observe that average speaking level may be modified by cultural influences "to a wide extent" and mention the case of Puerto Rican girls in New York City who "tend to speak on a rather high pitch". In contrast, "many American women ... find it desirable to speak on an artificially low pitch level".

Crystal (1975: 79) also raises the importance of variations in pitch-range between languages where "language or dialect A (uses) a higher overall range than B", for which Trudgill (1974: 186) provides an example: high rather than medium or deep pitch range is characteristic of working class Norwich speech — of both males and females. This high pitch level significantly distinguishes this sociolect from the speech associated with other socio-economic groups such as the rural East Anglian population and the middle class. However, like most non-syntactic aspects of pitch, investigations into these cultural variations are rare and statements concerning such phenomena are often imprecisely and impressionistically stated. However, Laver and Trudgill (1979) present the first full sociolinguistic treatment of phonetic markers in speech touching on various features such as tone of voice and pitch.

In order to put the results into an international sociolinguistic perspective it is necessary to briefly review the occasional references to social corre-

lates of pitch. Crystal (1975: 84) finds this the most neglected area of all prosodic studies and argues that prosodic features belong as much to social
speech styles as the articulation of vowels and consonants as well as grammatical inflections.

For instance, in Chichimeca, differences in a speaker's tone serve to
identify the addressee's sex (Driver and Driver 1963: 108); in Koasati, syllabic tone differences may distinguish between the sexes also (Haas 1944)
Adams (1957: 226) comments on the "subtle qualities of tone, pitch and
melody" in an Egyptian dialect, which are employed to establish status
between speakers; Gumperz (1964: 144) mentions an intimate style in
Khalapur characterized by pitch glides not occurring in the formal style;
Irvine (1975) states that one feature that differentiates noble Wolof speech-
style from low caste speech style is the use of low pitch by those of high rank
in contrast to the high pitch used by those of low status.

Unfortunately, few of these references have been the subject of intensive instrumental investigations and their validity is therefore questionable.
Nevertheless, to say that pitch phenomena have a social function as well as a
grammatical and semantic one is uncontroversial.

Let us now consider the relationship between femininity and language,
particularly with reference to suprasegmental phenomena. Of course, there
has been a multitude of studies dealing with sex differences in verbal communication recently; they have been conveniently summarized in an annotated bibliography by Henley and Thorne (1975).

The fact that women are generally politer in their speech than men has
been commented on by Lakoff (1975: 51-52). According to her now well-
known treatise, a woman must "dress decoratively, look attractive, be com-
pliant" in order to survive in society and these constraints are reflected in a
female's "overgentility of speech and etiquette" (1975: 27), in hyperformality
and hypercorrectness, statements with rising intonation, tag questions and
modifications such as 'I think', 'sort of' etc. Crosby and Nyquist (1977) generally support Lakoff's view in their investigation of American women's language and maintain that there are linguistic features that correspond to the
notion of 'speaking like a lady'. They could not, however, establish that this
style arose from the inferior status of women in society; instead they postulate
that sex differences in language are "due to role differentiation, rather than
to status differentiation" (ibid. p.321). As for the status and role of women in
Japan, Nakane (1970: 32) writes that Japanese women are almost always
ranked as inferiors. Apart from the lack of access to high status position, it

seems that Japanese women have to conform to specific role behaviour quite rigidly (De Vos 1973: 39-44). Lebra (1976: 87) interestingly notes:

> "sexuality for Japanese seems foremost a role concept. To be a woman means to play a woman's role in relation to others. Femininity thus may be consciously or deliberately displayed in external adornment as well as behaviour and *speech*" (my emphasis)

Pharr (1976: 306) also states:

> "Whereas in England romantic and chivalrous traditions had developed in the feudal era to soften the very real lines of status difference between men and women, in Japan with different feudal traditions the lines were very stark indeed. In the prewar period women showed deference to men of their own as well as higher classes through the use of polite language and honorific forms of address, bowing more deeply than men, walking behind their husbands in public, and in numerouus other ways deferring to men".

As discussed in Chapter 1 (section 1.3.2.1.) the Japanese language makes distinct syntactic and lexical distinctions between male and female language; honorific speech is also associated with femininity if not a marker of it.

Although Key (1972: 18) claims that "no linguistic study has ever indicated basic differences in male/female intonation patterns in English as, for example, we might find in vocabulary differences", two studies on the subject will be mentioned here. First of all, in her investigation into American English, Brend (1972: 868) found that "men consistently avoid certain intonation levels or patterns: they very rarely, if ever, use the highest level of pitch that women use" and that "there are differences in male and female intonation patterns (which) may be present in many more languages than those for which it has already been reported, and, indeed, may be present in all languages". Another study concerned with intonation contours and not pitch range, as is the case here, is Edelsky's (1979) investigation into the correlation between femininity and statements using a rising contour. Her findings are that the actual intonational production she studied failed to reveal sexual encoding; but there exist stereotype language attitudes which "reflect the differential social statuses of the sexes; and ... may ... also bear the burden of perpetuation" of that difference (Edelsky 1979: 30).

Further references that deserve citing in this connection are Farb (1973) who claims that an 'effeminate' voice in English has a wider pitch range than the male norm; Kramer (1974) who finds that high pitch is a stereotyped attribute of females and Sachs, Lieberman and Erickson (1973) who are surprised to discover that the acoustic differences between adult men and women are greater than their anatomical differences (larger larynx and vocal cords in the male) would lead one to expect since men have a tendency to talk as if they were bigger and women as though they were smaller than their actual physical structure.

4.1.5. *Concluding hypothesis*

What this study reveals is that pitch level in certain Japanese situations such as that of formal politeness as here serves to highlight sexual differences in a much more marked fashion than pitch level in English does in the same circumstances. In contrast to sharp Japanese sexual differentiation in English there seems to be sexual 'convergence' in pitch. The hypothesis postulated for this is as follows.

Japanese expectations of sexual and social role are much more rigid than those prescribed by English norms. In formal circumstances in which there is social equality between male speakers (as was indicated to the subjects before the recording and also reflected in the text given in note 134), Japanese males take a low profile linguistically, understating, being terse, presenting an unemotional, self-restrained exterior (Barnlund 1975; Lebra 1976). Consider also Seward's comments (1968: 111) that "Japanese men emphasize the masculinity of their speech by adopting a *deep-voiced*, *gutteral mode* of speaking which is often accompanied by stern faces and stiff postures" (my emphasis). This 'controlled' profile, it is suggested here, is reflected in the low pitch level of Japanese males in relation to English males of generally equivalent phonational limits. In contrast, the Japanese women in polite situations are expected to be very voluble, decorative and feminine in their speech (cf. Miller 1967: 289). This 'daintiness' is further emphasized, so the investigator believes, by what is clearly an artificially high pitch level, as indicated in this study's findings. These pitch contrasts become more salient when hearing the Japanese not employing polite formulae such as *arigatō gozaimasu*. Additionally, I have observed — but this requires empirical substantiation — how males in service situations e.g. shopkeepers and hotel staff and in other contexts in which males assume a conventionally inferior status, adopt a high pitch level, thereby employing a high pitch range metaphorically to suggest subservience.

Pitch differences between the sexes are less marked in English politeness formulae, because what English males are doing here is implying a low social status by aiming at a high pitch which, as Brown and Levinson (1978: 273) point out, has "natural associations with the voice quality of children" and, additionally of course, of women, both of whom traditionally occupy positions of lower status to males. The hypothesis suggested here is that there is some kind of deferential implication by the social associations of high pitch level[138] when English males use it. Such a view is surely not so incredible when it has been observed that low-caste speakers of Tamil address high-caste, powerful persons in a "customary thin high-pitched voice" (Brown and Levinson 1978: 272) or that Wolofs of the noble caste employ low pitch as one means of presenting themselves to others as dignified speakers of honour (Irvine 1975).

Synthesizing these two hypotheses for the Japanese and English data, the conclusion reached is that high pitch level is employed for distinctly different sociosemiotic functions in the two language communities. In Japan a high pitch level serves to express a stereotypically female role while among educated British English speakers high[139] pitch level is a means of signalling politeness adopted by both sexes and not only in situations of male inferiority.

4.2. Semiotic schism in Japanese-Western interaction

This final section considers problems in the decoding of comunicative behaviour occurring when the interacting participants do not share the same sociocultural framework for approaching and organizing 'reality', do not adhere to a similar set of beliefs and values and whose patterns of interactional signifying do not always match. Such cross-cultural miscoding or 'semiotic schism' can lead to considerable anxiety and frustration, possibly culminating in communication breakdown. The problem lies in the inability of either interactant to adequately and appropriately interpret the signals of a different sociocultural code for communication.

The insights and findings of various schools and fields are drawn upon here, including semiotics, sociolinguistics, social psychology, the ethnography of speaking, discourse and text analysis as well as applied linguistics[140]. The principal approach adopted, however, is semiotic and sociolinguistic since these perspectives directly handle the interactants' problems and concerns.

4.2.1. The concept 'semiotic schism'

A schism denotes a dissension or cleavage within an organized body. If we take interaction itself as a form of organization, no matter how temporary, then semiotic schism refers to the dissension between interactants' readings

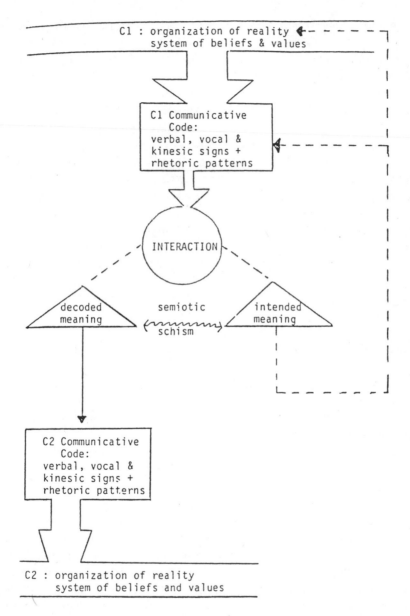

Fig. 4   *Semiotic schism*: the process of cross-cultural miscoding. (C1 refers to the cultural system of the sender and C2 to the different cultural system of the receiver-decoder.)

of each other. This section, however, does not represent the work of a schismatist[141] but aims at overcoming semiotic asynchrony in cross-cultural transactions and, by explaining the phenomenon (with the aid of Japanese data) points to its potential resolution.

Semiotic schism appears to be something interactants are not consciously aware of, although they may acknowledge each other's cultural differences on an abstract level. The fact that these differences are expressed symbolically in a different communicative code is rarely recognized. Participants readily believe in the accuracy of their 'readings' of another's communicative signs where these same signs appear in their own culture. Often if misunderstandings occur, they are not attributed to incorrect decoding but to the personality and attitudes of the culturally different interlocutor and the community to which he/she belongs; negative stereotyping and its perpetual reinforcement is one consequence. Thus, it is essential to raise the cross-cultural interactants' level of awareness of erroneous decoding. When access to the interpretation of another's communicative code is not available, an initial suspension of decoding activity i.e. no initial judging, is advisable; this, of course, requires considerable open-mindedness and tolerance from the participants. Non-native cultural communication should not be instantly equated in the same semiotic way as the verbal and non-verbal behaviour of one's own culture. This semiotic openness cannot develop when the cross-cultural communication take place in a context of imbalance, be it social, political — or even psychological[142]. Where uncertainty, suspicion or potential mistrust underlie participants' communication, the chances of successful cross-cultural decoding are greatly reduced.

Fig.4. represents in diagram form the process of semiotic schism. Each culture has its own methods of organizing reality, its particular constellation of beliefs and values with their implicit norms and conventions, its historically transmitted but also adaptive and creative ethos as well as its symbols of dress, food, architecture and communication[143]. The latter is its communicative code which can be analyzed into two sub-systems: verbal, vocal and kinesic signs, on the one hand, and rhetoric patterns on the other. Rhetoric patterns refer to the principles and conventions which connect, compose and regulate symbolizing behaviour but whose function is not primarily symbolic itself. For communication should be understood as constituted by two simultaneous but separate systems: one symbolizing and the other organizing (cf. Loveday 1983). There are phonological, grammatical, lexical, pragmatic/discoursal/textual symbols or VERBAL SIGNS as well as the symbols produced by the vocal organs themselves e.g. volume, pitch, speed and voice quality which are VOCAL SIGNS. Additionally, gestures of the body and face, posture and the use of interpersonal space also signify and are here referred to as KINESIC SIGNS. However, rhetoric patterns do come to be invested with meaning, deriving from the effect or manner of their assembling and employment in terms of the community's value system and can be treated semiotically. They are taken as indications of interactants' motives, abilities, personality and sophistication among others. Of course, interaction itself generates all these signs at once and it is up to the receiver to decode as appropriately as he can the intended (and unintended) meanings[144]. From the dotted lines in Fig.4. we can see how a native sharing the same sociocultural communicative code as the sender would be able to appropriately decode the intended meaning by relating it back to his knowledge of the code and native culture. The native culture (of the sender) is referred to as C1 and is comparable to the notion of a first, native language or L1. However, the receiver from a different culture, C2, who is unfamiliar with the C1 communicative code, miscodes the intended meaning by relating it to the C2 code and cultural system, producing semiotic schism. If the two triangles representing the intended and decoded meaning of an interactant's behaviour converge and overlap, interaction will obviously proceed more smoothly with minimal or no interpretive conflict. There will be a greater sense of mutuality and coopertion; more favourable attitudes will be fostered. In contrast, if semiotic schism persists over a period of or throughout the interaction, confusion, anxiety, discomfort or even hostility may arise.

Finally, it is important to emphasize that meaning is, of course, something dynamic, contextually defined and mutually negotiated. There is nothing inherently meaningful in the sign itself; meaning derives from how an interactant has learnt or chosen to value it (cf. Brown and Fraser 1979). An interactional sign can be produced for a multitude of purposes and likewise receive a multitude of ascribable values. Since the focus of this section is on the negative consequences in cross-cultural communication of interpersonal attribution[145] arising from inaccurate decoding of C1 interactional signs by C2 members, the study concerns itself only with those signs in Japanese-Western transactions which have been observed as directly part of the process of semiotic schism.

4.2.2. The Japanese case

The basic line of approach here is to view the C1 as Japanese and the C1 communicative code also as that of Japan. The term 'Western' is applied to

the C2 decoder but requires some explanation. It is used to refer to the North European cultural and communicative framework which also holds for certain groups of North Americans, e.g. WASPs. This may appear a gross and imprecise generalization but nevertheless is usually recognized as 'serviceable' despite variations within these countries and their communities. The context of cross-cultural communication focussed on here could be any of the following:
– Japanese communicating in English in Japan with Westerners
– Japanese communicating in English in the West with Westerners
– Japanese communicating in Japanese in Japan with Westerners who are unfamiliar with the Japanese communicative code

Mention, however, of the Japanese interpretation of Western communicative behaviour will also be made. Only Japanese-Western encounters and transactions of a more formal and public nature i.e. non-intimate, will be discussed since in intimate or familiar contexts semiotic schism is less likely to occur due to the established solidarity and the accompanying interpretive openness of the participants, although miscoding may also arise here too.

From Fig.4. it is clear that the communicative code issues from and depends on the cultural system which developed and operates it. Therefore, it would be impossible to forgo even the briefest outline of the principal themes of Japanese culture which orientate and steer the verbal, vocal and kinesic signs together with the rhetoric patterns.

Lebra (1976) provides an extensive account of fundamental features of Japanese culture, often illustrated by communicative behaviour; the underlying sociocultural principles of the Japanese which Lebra presents are social relativism, a sense of belongingness, empathy, dependency, reciprocity and hierarchical identification[146]. Hioki (1981) offers an analysis of Japanese norms and values and demonstrates how these are expressed in the communicative code. Hioki pinpoints seven postulates which all derive from key words and phrases in Japanese:

1. respect for seniority (*chōyō no jo*[147])
2. politeness (*keigo*)
3. communal responsibility (*rentaikan*) and sensitivity to face (*kao*)
4. inner versus outer worlds (*uchi to soto*)
5. modesty (*hikaeme*)
6. the resolution of conflict by peaceful means (*maruku osameru*)
7. abandonment of individual self and collective identification (*shōga o sute taiga o toru*)

These abstract social values will appear in the following discussion. It is not possible to give a summary of research on Japanese culture within the limitations of this chapter, although it is clearly only against this background that communicative behaviour of a community can be adequately explicated. For further references, see Benedict (1946), Nakane (1970) and Doi (1973).

4.2.3. *Decoding Japanese-Western interaction*

Without doubt, a certain amount of individual variation in the employment and interpretation of communicative signs and rhetoric patterns exists within a community as well as when interpreting communication outside that community. This variation may be related to the sex, age, social background, occupation, health and other conditions of the individual sign producer. Furthermore, the signs produced adapt to and evolve differently according to particular contexts. Both these facts may render generalizations about the use and decoding of cross-cultural interaction signs invalid. However, if the community itself did not have access to some covert, shared and generalizable scheme of interpretation, how could it account for its members' communicative behaviour? The very survival of the community depends on its communicational interpretability. Thus, the principle of semiotic generalization is justifiable from an ethnomethodological and ecological viewpoint.

The data which follows has been drawn from various sources. Some has been recorded academically while other parts derive from first-hand observation and participation in cross-cultural interaction. Comments and discussion with others involved in such transactions have also contributed. Some of the data is necessarily impressionistic and open to the criticism of subjectivity and thus requires subsequent verification.

4.2.3.1. *Verbal signs*

Verbal signs are specifically linguistic in their nature and are constituted by that traditional unit of the word. Here, a verbal sign may be a lexeme, a grammatical structure or phrase or a sentence/utterance bearing semantic, pragmatic or sociolinguistic values.

The aim here is not to provide an exhaustive catalogue of cross-cultural miscoding in J-W interaction (from now on J will stand for Japanese, W for Western and E for English) but to provide a variety of examples which highlight the process of semiotic schism in its many facets.

The words *yes/no* take on different interpretations in W and J cultures; J interactants tend to use 'yes' merely as a signal of listenership and not necessarily to express agreement with the propositional content of an interlocutor.

A typical example of the confusion such simple but significantly differential decoding is recorded by Seward (1976: 36)

> "Often at conferences attended by American and Japanese businessmen, I have heard chilling exchanges like this:
> American Camera Importer (speaking through interpreter): 'Can you ship by the end of this month?'
> Japanese Camera Manufacturer: 'Hai, raigetsu no hatsuka goro shukka dekimasu'.
> (lit. Yes, we can ship about the 20th of next month.)
> The American, knowing enough Japanese to think that he knows that *hai* means yes, smiled brightly when he heard the word *hai*, but this reaction switched to puzzlement and then irritation when the interpreter went on to explain that the shipment would be effected around the twentieth of next month".

The word 'no' also requires interpretation. Its J counterpart comes close to abuse. Ueda (1974) discovered that it is only among family members in the home that the J use 'no', while in public "exiting, lying or equivocation is preferred" (1974: 192). In W speech- communities, on the other hand, the occurrence of 'no' and with it the expression of disagreement is not considered so damaging to interaction. This can have various repercussions in cross-cultural communication. For example, a J begins a conversation with a native C2 E speaker by making some trivial comment about a particular subject. His E interlocutor cuts in with "Oh no, I think ..." resulting in the J speaker's subsequent silence for the rest of what will probably be a very limited exchange. Another possible scenario could be that of an E speaker ringing up a J to ask if the latter can meet him in town at a certain time. Due to some other commitment or whatsoever, the J cannot go but does not decline bluntly with 'no'; his exiting is interpreted by the C2 interactant as constituting an agreement to the arrangement but when he/she does not turn up the blame is attached to the C1 sign-maker and not the faulty C2 decoder.

Moving from this microlevel, let us turn to the verbal expression of gratitude for which Doi (1973: 11) gives a personal illustration of semiotic schism:

> "during my early days in America — when a psychiatrist who was my supervisor did me some kindness or other — I have forgotten exactly what, but it was something quite trivial. Either way, feeling the need to say something, I produced not 'thank you', as one might expect, but 'I'm sorry'. 'What are you sorry for?' he replied promptly, giving me an odd look. I was highly embarassed. My difficulty in saying 'thank you' arose, I imagine, from a feeling that it implied too great an equality with someone who was in fact my

superior. In Japanese, I suppose I should have said *domo arigato gozaimasu* or *domo sumimasen*, but unable to express the same feeling of obligation in English, I had come up with 'I am sorry' as the nearest equivalent".

Coulmas (1981a: 89) contrastively analyses J and W speech acts of gratitude and respect and concludes thus:

> "under the effect of an ethics of indebtedness, the Japanese tend to equate gratitude with a feeling of guilt. Apology expressions seem to be the most appropriate means to meet the resultant requirements. Accordingly, Japanese verbal behaviour exhibits an exquisite sensitivity to mutual obligations, responsibility and moral indebtedness"

Differences in the Japanese address system (cf. flowchart in ch.1. section 1.2.2.), with the signs closely referring to age and status grading and sexual differentiation, also can lead to initial cross-cultural miscoding. The increasing W tendency towards first naming, if applied to the J context, carries the implication of intimacy or inferiority if it is not reciprocal. Westerners in Japan are frequently heard voicing their dislike of what they have interpreted as an overdifferentiated sense of social hierarchy and collective identification. J interactants may introduce themselves as "I belong to Mitsubishi bank" and seek to establish the collective affiliations of their W communicators by immediately asking seemingly offensive questions such as "Where do you work?" and (for status and age ranking) "How old are you?"[148]

The success of cross-cultural communication in formal transactions relies heavily on the accurate decoding of politeness strategies[149]. However, as Scarcella's and Brunak's study (1981) of speaking politely in a second language concludes, low-level L2 speakers show much less variety in the politeness strategies they use and lack any apparent variation of politeness features. Although based on universal principles, Brown and Levinson (1978) do state that cultures select from universal possibilities certain preferred styles and strategies for expressing politeness and that the motivation for this selection tends to be obscure. It is my general impression that when communicating with non-Japanese in Japan, the J tend to apply positive politeness strategies[150] if they are not familiarized with or confident about interaction with Westerners. Positive politeness strategies might, at first sight, appear an unlikely choice in the case of J-W interaction but the J folk-linguistically believe that W communication tends to be generally relaxed and informal. Furthermore, they do not wish interaction to become hardened or blocked by limited routines expressed with respectful rigidity as is the norm for J negative politeness strategies. Additionally, they presume, working on the basis of cultural expectations, that the W interactant will play along as ascribed 'friend' or ingroup member cf. note 150. The problem is that positive politeness strategies work on the assumption that the Speaker and Hearer both consider each other as similar, even though this may only be for the sake of successfully completing the transaction. If cross-cultural interactants' conceptions as to their relative 'similarity' and 'equality' diverge, then positive politeness strategies are interpretable as demeaning and insulting, usually leading to an early termination of the encounter. If J interactants apply their C1 negative politeness strategies which can involve convoluting expressions of vagueness and indirectness (cf. 4.2.3.4. below), including long pauses, little kinesic accompaniment and so on, Westerners may also interpret these interactional signs as rudely evasive and highly artificial or even hollow (cf. Miller (1970: 289-290) who gives an example of what can seem to Westerners as exaggerated J negative politeness).

The problem seems to lie in the inavailability or non-operation in the J communicative code of a semi-formal, middle level of politeness; in other words, the extremes of negative or positive politeness hold sway in the J speech-community[151]. Interestingly enough, Ogasawara (1972) states that whereas the J politeness axis is vertical and based on status/age inferiority versus superiority, the W politeness axis is horizontal. Equally, Westerners inept at the C1 communicative code, can just as equally damage cross-cultural interaction by applying positive politeness strategies:

> "Thinking to cement beyond the point of any possible future rupture the bonds of Japanese-American friendship in general and those ligatures that wedded his company to (the president of a Japanese partner company, a young American businessman who had been in Japan only for several months, attending a particular cocktail party) determined to break down the barriers of reserve that stood between his and this forbidding gentleman (Mr Doi) by cheerfully saying to him something like, 'Good to see you, Doi, you ole son of a gun!'
> Having plotted this strategy and selected from his scant stock those Japanese words that might convey an approximately similar meaning, he gulped down his third martini, approached the stern presence, clapped him heartily on the back, a gesture in itself offensive to most Japanese in general and to our Mr Doi in particular, and, winking largely said in a clear, ringing voice: '*Kora, Doi, takusan sukebei hanchosan, ne!*' (fairly literally: Hey, Doi, you're a lecherous boss, aren't you?) Mr Doi's face turned ashen gray and he stalked out of the party. Within two days, he had made representations to the president of the U.S. company to have our well-meaning young American sent

home — or any place except Japan — and he was successful in this'. (Seward 1976: 123)

In an informal context, this positive politeness strategy might have proven successful.

4.2.3.2. *Vocal signs*

Another dimension of semiotic schism occurs on the phonetic level of communication. Of course, the usual difficulties in perceiving and reproducing sounds of a non-native language are bound to hamper cross-linguistic communicators, depending on the degree of phonological interference[152] of the L2 speaker. Since Japanese has only five vowels and thirteen consonants while certain English varieties can have as many as twenty[153] vowels and twenty four consonants, the gravest interference (cf. section 4.1.2. above), is produced on the Japanese side. Such interference in itself should not lead to semiotic schism. It may lead to non-comprehension of parts or all of the J speaker's message. It may also contribute to a feeling of distance by giving ground for a negative evaluation by a native speaker of the linguistic ability of his interlocutor and could evoke the negative, stereotypical images transmitted in media, jokes and by hearsay of the particular foreign group. Various studies have shown that it is generally not the L2 grammar nor the command of L2 educated vocabulary that seems to carry most significance for the L1 community but the native-likeness of the L2 speaker's accent; the closer it sounds to the community's pronunciation, the more favourably regarded and more easily accepted the non-native will be (cf. Giles 1978). According to Williams (1970) reactions to speech can be linked to a set of beliefs providing stereotypes which influence the listener's behaviour and thereby become social reality. Thus, a strong L2 accent of an Oriental may generate unfavourable perceptions in terms of empathy, attractiveness and sophistication or even constitute a basis for 'foreigner talk'[154] (cf. Snow et al. 1981).

Training and practice may overcome the negative aesthetics and social categorizing elicited by 'thick' L2 accents but much harder to eradicate and interpret are the signs evoked by L1 suprasegmental features and voice quality. Similarly, these are the most difficult to interpret appropriately in cross-cultural communication.

As the investigation into the pitch correlates of politeness formulae produced by J and E informants of both sexes described above in section 4.1. demonstrates, significant pitch differences between J and E speakers when expressing politeness may lead to cross-cultural miscoding with the low pitch performance of J males in polite E contexts interpretable as a lack of interest and involvement in the interaction and interactant and implying rudeness. Related to this are the comments of Cammack and van Buren (1967) who note that when J speakers and especially women transfer their voice quality setting for politeness contexts to non-native or cross-cultural contexts, the symbolization is not one of deference and distance as in J but of extreme intimacy as in private male-female relations and of feminine baby-talk usually associated with a lack of intelligence. The voice quality in question is composed of breathiness, openness, lowered volume and raised register. The authors go on to point out that female E speakers "often sound harsh, raucous, rude or overly masculine to a Japanese ear" (1967: 8).

Other aspects of semiotic schism linked to voice quality in J-W interaction are the contradicting attitudes towards nasality. If J females are nasal and high-pitched, they are considered dainty and coquettish. Scherer (1979: 183) discovered, however, that nasalization in E females is considered "unattractive, foolish, lethargic and self effacing".

Japanese speech speeds are also differently evaluated: the J take slow speaking as an indication of prudence and thoughtfulness; Westerners react to this slow pace with frustration and impatience. J volume tends to be either much louder or softer than that of E-using communities, resulting in impressions of lack of respect, roughness or, if very soft, introversion and extreme shyness. In fact, J loud volume[155], often accompanied by heavy stressing and repetition, occurs usually in public transactions to indicate interpersonal amenability, respect and interactional security. Soft volume, although also a sign of respect, may be considered suspicious and inappropriate for public contexts. Lip-puckering or labiality[156] is used by J to indicate affection and solidarity; Westerners may feel as if they are being viewed as 'incompetent infants' or spoken down to when this occurs, since this voice setting is reserved for baby-talk in their community and not appropriate among adults. One of the most frequent vocal sounds issuing from interaction with J is laughter — in every variation from titter to giggle to chuckle, snigger and falsetto cackle. Although initially charmed, the Westerner frequently comes to question the raison d'être of speech continually interspersed with laughter. Is the J interlocutor really trying to act like an immature schoolchild? For the J community, laughter serves (together with smiling discussed below) as an essential component of a pleasant and even formal encounter. It binds interactants in a non-linguistic manner which is highly appreciated in the J speech-community where words are rarely trusted and also functions as an important 'release valve' for the tension built up by restraint and rigid politeness. It also serves to soften and 'humanize' the latter.

Furthermore, J do not hesitate and certain individuals seem even to cultivate punctiliar physiological acts which (for Westerners) interrupt polite interaction such as continually clearing the throat, gulping, yawning, sighing, scratching, sniffing and stretching. The resulting vocal sounds seem to add to the personal nature of the exchange and allow for the interlocutor to relax for a moment and then re-focus better on interaction; they carry no negative connotations. Westerners, on the other hand, try to cancel out as much of this extralinguistic physicalness from their communication and interpret J who punctuate their speaking, if in formal contexts, with such acts as purposefully slowing down or 'turning off' the transaction and as potentially insulting since it seems to suggest 'carelessness' and a 'lack of respect' on the part of the performer unless obviously unavoidable.

4.2.3.3. *Kinesic signs*

In 4.2.3.2. above smiling, a form of kinesic behaviour, has already been referred to. It is essential to realize that the maintenance of interaction is crucially dependent upon the interactants' abilities to establish a rhythmic exchange of turn-taking and content-commenting through signals such as gaze direction, head nods, smiles, eye blinks, facial gestures and so forth. Erikson's (1973) study between different ethnic groups speaking the same language (English) shows that the successful ability to establish and continue this rhythmic exchange in interaction depends on a *shared* ethnic background.

Kinesic signs co-occur and usually support the linguistic signs in communication but the further systems semiotically operate from each other, the greater the chances of semiotic schism. This is particularly dangerous since the kinesic channel constitutes the basis of interactional activity.

It is impossible to fully handle this area here and only a few examples will have to suffice. As yet no generally recognized classificatory or analytical framework for kinesic behaviour exists; here that of Ekman and Friesen (1969) guides the following account.

Emblems or sign language are probably the least disturbing symbols even when not amenable to direct, cross-cultural interpretation since they are so clearly unattributable to interactants' personality or attitudes in a direct way. Saint-Jacques (1972) has described a stock of Japanese emblems e.g. the circle made with index finger and thumb signifying 'money' among J but

'OK, good or delicious' among Westerners; the calling of a person towards oneself by J is accomplished by extending the arm upwards, palm downwards and moving the fingers (or the whole hand) rapidly up and down which Westerners may take as a signal meaning 'go away' or 'goodbye'. Neither do differences in illustrators, the movements which illustrate a speaker's informational content, seem to seriously disturb or rupture cross-cultural communication although they may be considered odd and irrelevant. However, this cannot be said of regulators which maintain and control turn-taking, signalling to the speaker to continue, repeat, elaborate, hurry up or become more explicit, for example. The initiation and termination of interaction can also be indicated via kinesic regulators i.e. bowing in the J context or handshaking in the W. According to Knapp (1978: 17):

> "regulators seem to be on the periphery of our awareness and are generally difficult to inhibit. They are like overlearned habits and are almost involuntary, but we are very much aware of these signals sent by others".

As already mentioned, smiling and also nodding are significant J regulators. The face and its displays are very important also in this respect. In Japan self-control is highly valued and the ideal of a deadpan face in situations of great anxiety was strongly promoted by the Samurai ethos cf. the following lesson from an early 18th century guide for the samurai which, even though 200 years old, still holds as an ideal of masculine kinesics today:

> "one's appearance bespeaks dignity corresponding to the depth of his character. One's concentrated effort, serene attitude, taciturn air, courteous disposition, thoroughly polite bearing, gritted teeth with a piercing look — each of these reveals dignity. Such outward appearance, in short, comes from constant attentiveness and seriousness". (Tsunetomo 1980: 95)

Such expressionless in J-W interaction may be taken as coldness or lack of interpersonal interest instead of its C1 meaning of dignity and seriousness. Contrastingly, J tend to react to the comparatively greater amount of W facial movement with amusement, considering them as evidence of pantomimic skills and not sincere expressions. Although Cuceloglu's work (1967) demonstrates that facial signalling movements are in no manner universally interpretable, it should be noted that *natural* facial expressions are. The problem arises in the appropriate decoding of the culturally acquired movements and the manipulation and controlling of movements. Frowning, for example, can indicate among Westerners a serious response to interactional content but indicates disapproval or anger to the J.

Eye movement receives heavy semiotic value in the J community, since the rest of the face is more or less immobile. A special study of the subject is clearly warranted but a few points deserve mention. While many W societies regard a person as slightly suspicious or shifty if he does not make a certain amount of eye contact with his partner when talking face to face, the J tend not to look straight into a person's eyes when talking in formal or public contexts[157] as this is perceived as threatening and rude; it is also part of the rules for a modest presentation of self (cf. Hioki's postulate No.5). Westerners miscode this J tendency to look down or away from their interlocutors as symbolic of guilt or shame or submission; in turn, Westerners, intent on signalling their earnestness and openness through eye contact, are perceived as provocative violators of personal respect. This means that J-W cross-cultural interactants rarely achieve smooth turn-taking because their mutual gazing does not correspond and interrelate with the interaction; the J tend to look down at the end of a turn which seems to suggest disavowal of social contact to the W who is used to continual gazing at the end of a turn which is necessary for the listener's assumption of the speaking rights. Where the speaker does not yield a speaking turn by gazing at the other, the listener will probably delay response and possibly not respond at all. However, it should be realized that in informal and intimate contexts the exact opposite is true: the Japanese may intensively fix their eyes on the interlocutor's which may be variously interpreted as, for example, 'childish' or 'seductive' or even 'rude'.

These J eye movements are accompanied by smiling, which may indicate amicability and politeness towards the interlocutor but, if prolonged, tends to be miscoded by Westerners who find the extensive smiling as unwarranted, undermining trust and even suggestive of deceitfulness. Klineberg (1935: 285-286) writes of this enigmatic J kinesic sign:

> "the Japanese smile is not necessarily a spontaneous expression of amusement, but a law of etiquette, elaborated and cultivated from early times. It is a silent language, often seemingly inexplicable to Europeans, and it may arouse violent anger in them as a consequence".

For Miller (1967: 288) smiling in Japan is:

> "not traditionally associated with good humour or a friendly attitude but rather with embarassment and social discomfort, or even, in extreme instances with genuine tragedy and sorrow, or with repressed anger".

Key (1975: 89) interestingly notes "the irresolvable conflict" of a J stewardess on an overseas airline "in greeting passengers with a traditional Japanese polite phrase, which would require a poker face, and at the same time manifesting the warm hospitality of the West, which requires a winning smile".

The negative W interpretation of certain J female alter-adaptors[158] has been analysed by Ramsey (1981). These adaptors have to do with covering behaviour to prevent a receiver from seeing the interactant's mouth, nose and cheek areas. This is achieved with the partial or total covering of hand(s) over the mouth or the use of an object or even another person to hide behind. Ramsay calls this 'cut-off' behaviour since it blocks various amounts of primary visual stimuli. This behaviour is found in many cultures and associated with flirting, embarassment and coyness but in Japan is heavily emphasized and culturally valued as part of a woman's self-representation, acting "as a kind of social releaser which elicits desired (favourable) feelings" (1981: 115) from other interactants, usually resulting in the performer's gaining approval or 'getting their way'. However, both male and female non-Japanese in the study did not have favourable impressions of J women using such cut-off adaptors. "Perceptions such as 'they look silly and childish' were commonly heard" (1981: 115). Cf. "When I saw her the first time she seemed so confident and mature. Her hand on her mouth really changed my feeling — she became so immature and childish" (1981: 121). The semiotic schism arises here due to the fact that this kinesic symbol is generally reserved in the W uniquely for children, often occurring in peek-a-boo games, and its use in adulthood is interpreted as affected, "less polite" and "less proper" (1981: 122). Moreover, Ramsey concludes: "It is reasonable also to expect that lack of such behaviours in kind, by non-Japanese, could be cause for negative perceptions by Japanese" (1981: 122).

Posture plays an important role in interaction (cf. Sheflen (1972) who estimates that there are about 30 culturally standard postural configurations of shared communicative significance for Americans, each occurring in a limited number of contexts). Postural style varies in relation to the sex, age, status, occupation, health and personality traits of interactants. Postural congruence is a symbol of mutuality and when it is absent in a totally native context, it signifies the non-association of the participants. In cross-cultural contexts, it is a very fundamental indicator of the evolution and success of the transaction.

The J kinesic norm of self control in formal situations appears to Westerners as extreme physical rigidity or even motionlessness; it is typically composed of a straight back with hardly any shifting. Kawasaki (1970: 155) comparatively notes:

"The Japanese is not demonstrative; on the contrary he tends to repress his feelings, and in a given situation tends to recoil upon himself. A Westerner will loll in a chair with his legs flung out before him, while a Japanese kneels down and sits on his heels".

Space between people and objects can symbolize and proxemic miscoding in cross-cultural communication is all too common. Hall (1972) claims that American space judgements depend principally on the tactile (body contact during interaction) and visual senses, although body odour and heat as well as the oral-aural systems are also involved. There exist two commonly observed levels of American spatial proximity in contexts defined as 'casual-personal' and 'social-consultative' which are four and twelve feet respectively. These represent the absolute extreme distances of closeness and remoteness. In Japan the casual-personal is only a few inches apart if at all since body contact is not tabooed. In public contexts such as train travel, the J do not shun body contact while Westerners consciously avoid it which makes Westerners in J react with anxiety at having their personal sense of space invaded by strangers. The social-consultative distance in Japan can be fifteen or more feet. The potential for misunderstanding is evident; offence arising in both contexts and in both cultures is inevitable: Westerners are seen in intimate settings as strangely distant while the J as uncomfortably close physically; in formal settings, Westerners are seen as rudely close because they do not respect greater distance while the J are interpreted as remote or even 'prejudiced' for not stepping a few feet closer. Related to this is the J tendency to walk slightly behind an interactant who is judged as socially superior; a wife may walk as much as five or six feet behind her husband in the street if she is traditional. Westerners who do not understand this proxemic sign become worried or frustrated at the seeming 'lurking' of the interactant behind them.

Proxemic meaning is obviously vital for fostering rappport, indicating the level of personal involvement and defining the nature of a relationship. Mizutani (1981: 40) provides an interesting illustration of his experience as a teacher of non-Japanese in America:

"When I had finished my first hour of teaching and was preparing to leave the classroom, an American coed called out to me. She was taller than me and looked quite imposing to me as she started walking to me. As I watched, she came closer and closer until it seemed that I would touch her if I raised my hand. It was my first class and I had no confidence about how it had gone so that, even though she did not look angry, I wondered if she might not be going to complain about something. Her facial expression was not all that

forbidding, but she came so close to me that I involuntarily took a step back-
ward. But when I did that she took another step closer to me. I felt like I was
being pursued by that tall student towering over me, and I retreated a second
time. However, the blackboard was behind me so that I could not withdraw
any further. I felt uneasy and made an effort to smile ... But she obviously
moved closer once again and said that she had a question. ... This experience
was an unsettling one for me because the distance between us was much
shorter than that normal between a Japanese man and woman".

Since the verbal articulation of thoughts and feelings in Japan is not
regarded as positively and admiringly as in the West, the kinesic channel
takes on extra significance. Various historical factors have contributed to this
non-verbalness: Japan's self-imposed island isolation, Zen and Buddhist
teachings which emphasize the value of silent reflection and two and half centuries of extreme societal control under the Tokugawa shogunate during
which time interaction was regulated right down to the exact manner of smiling to superiors[159]. The fascist period during this century presented another
version of this totalitarianism and, although chronologically limited, its social
consequences are still tangible and have yet to be fully appreciated.
The J have long been labelled as 'inscrutable Orientals', their communicative
world shrouded in mystery, suspicion and supposed impenetrability. On the
other hand, to the Japanese, Western kinesics have appeared as 'crude' and
'exaggerated' or 'lacking in restraint' and it still seems that neither Japan nor
the West has yet learned to accurately understand each other's body language. This is mainly due to the fact that the Japanese prefer to reduce self-
expression (and self-revelation) in public and formal situations to a much
greater extent than Westerners do (cf. Barnlund 1975). In cross-cultural
semiotics, the stereotypes and accompanying discomfort and stress in interaction emerge from the inability of either side to pick up the correct meaning of
the kinesic and other signs communicated. A much greater effort at interpretive tolerance and positiveness is vital for the successful outcome of intercultural exchanges.

4.2.3.4. *Rhetoric patterns*

Rhetoric patterns (cf. Loveday 1983) refer to the external and internal
structuring of texts on the suprasentential and -utterance level. These patterns are closely tied to the sociocultural framework in which they are operative. They can be classified into two types: (i) patterns for structuring interpersonal conduct and (ii) patterns for structuring verbal content. The former
are directly related to the social presentation of an interactant while the latter

type, although also frequently taken as important clues to interpreting an interactant's personal characteristics, are not primarily designed for the social expression of self but for the packing of information to be transmitted.

As for interaction-structuring patterns, we can easily observe cases of conflicting procedures for regulating interaction. Norms of quantity or the amount of speech necessary for appropriate and successful contact vary across speech-communities. As Kunihiro (1975: 97) states:

> "language as an instrument of debate or argument is considered ... disagreeable and is accordingly avoided ... It is only one possible means of communication, not *the* means of communication as is often the case among English speakers".

Verbal expression in Japan has not received the same emphasis as in the West where the importance of the spoken form was established by the Greek cultivation of public speaking into the art of rhetoric. Numerous J proverbs extol the virtues of shutting up cf. note 46. Unlike Westerners J do not feel uncomfortable if nothing is said for some time during interaction. Nakane (1972: 70) tells of the experience of an American teacher who could not bear the silence of the school staff room. Her colleagues, on the other hand, found it pleasant and comfortable.

This J rhetoric pattern of less verbal quantity can result in their being regarded by Westerners as "distant", "cool" and "cautious" and conversations with J considered as "endless and pointless" (Barnlund 1975. 56) while the J interpret what appears to them as excessive verbalization on the Westerner's part equally negatively, e.g.

> "... when I went to the United States in 1950 I was greatly surprised, almost perturbed, by the fact that Americans loved to talk incessantly. They even did so during the meal. As a matter of fact they sounded to me almost hypermanic". (Doi 1974: 21)

That for certain speech-communities silence is distressful while for others it is normal and pleasant relates to the value system which lays the foundations for rhetoric patterns.

The patterns for interactional partnership or consonance may also vary across cultures. In the J community, there is a much more extensive employment of listener signals, than in the West; cf. English 'mm', 'yeah', 'uh-uh', J tend to respond immediately after minimal utterances of the speaker, timing their responses to coincide either with the last syllable of an intonation group or with the pause preceding the next group: "the listener's constant participation creates a more intensely cooperative interaction than is typical of conversation in American English ... some English speakers addressing Japanese listeners may find themselves reduced to paralyzed silence by the barrage of verbal response and nodding which greet their words and seems to indicate that they have already been understood when they have scarcely begun to speak" (Clancy 1982: 74)

Of course, this apparent "barrage" is one way the J indicate willingness to enter into interaction as well as demonstrating their readiness to assume a listener role but W may have the impression of being treated as a handicapped person. On the other hand, J may feel insecure when a W partner does not provide frequent listener signals and interpret their absence as indicative of disagreement or unwillingness to pursue interaction.

Mizutani (1981: 83) claims that the taking and timing of turns is shorter in the J speech community where "a conversation is thought to be created together by two persons. It is even possible to speak with an intonation calling for *aizuchi* (listener signals) from the other person after a single word". As a result of this rhetoric pattern for structuring interpersonal conduct, Westerners often seem unable to respond appropriately in Japanese, "even those quite advanced in their study of Japanese ... feel somewhat out of step" due to the different expectations of utterance length and other timing-related phenomena. For instance, the J wait three seconds or longer before taking up the floor in conversation where ideas or information are seriously expressed while the W tends to interpret the pause as a sign for him to continue, being accustomed to a quicker pick up. The J then may continue to wait his regular length of time only to find that he cannot have an opportunity to make his conversational contribution.

One particularly important set of rhetoric patterns are formulistic routines which refer to the fixed, prefabricated phrases in communication such as greeting, leave-taking, apologizing, thanking, congratulating, stumbling, cursing, introducing and so on. Routine formulae play a fundamental role in the establishing and context-defining of interaction as well as expressing social relationships (cf. Coulmas 1981b). In the J community the use of ceremonial formulae are an integral part of daily behaviour. They are uttered without individual variation or alteration; there is no requirement for their 'personalization' as in W communities. Goldstein and Tamura (1975: 95) point out that

> "the form is not regarded as a barrier to expression of the self but is rather the technique by which two selves are connected in standard intercourse — meaning must then be inserted below or beyond the words. The idea of cliché is absent in the J world".

The semiotic schism here is when Westerners take the uttering of such formulae as artificial and affected since little or no personal comment is detectable[160].

> "To the American, the J method of standard messages, such as *congratulations* with only a name, the presentation of a gift with a standard phrase, a refusal with a standard phrase before acceptance ... may seem very bare indeed and perhaps somewhat insincere. The American may wonder if the giver or receiver really believes what he is saying ... Words must be personally manipulated by the American speaker to create the impression of himself, his feelings, and the connection between himself and the hearer that he wishes to give". (Goldstein and Tamura 1975: 91)

Either cross-cultural interactant must realize their community variance in the production of routines, believing in each other's sincerity. For the J, the Westerner's overindividualized expression also lacks credibility and seems to suggest wild abandon, social carelessness or shallow flamboyance.

The second set of rhetoric patterns which deal with the internal assembly of discourse are those for structuring verbal content. Their main aim is to negotiate sense in accordance with culturally defined values and beliefs. The emphasis on verbalness in the W has already been stated; this verbalness tends to be accompanied by, what J consider as, elaborate and unnecessary explicitness. For the community, precise and ordered talk is considered odd and even 'anti-social'; instead vagueness, hesitation, indirectness and 'incompleteness' are felt to be appropriate rhetoric patterns for organizing verbal content[161].

A J will rarely commit himself totally either way to a subject. He prefers to examine a proposition from as many angles as possible and with a great deal of tentativeness. In fact, as we have already noted, the J conception of what constitutes a complete utterance or sentence differs considerably from the W. It is generally regarded as unrefined to clearly mark the end of one's utterances and so the ending is frequently left hanging with a word like 'nevertheless' (*keredo ... ga*).

The semiotic schism resulting from the two different rhetoric patterns of vagueness versus directness produces attributions such as 'slippery' and 'double-dealing' from the W and 'arrogant' and 'aggressive' from the J.

Topic selection or what interactants choose to talk about may also be considered a rhetoric pattern of a kind. Barnlund (1975: 88) discovered that

> "Japanese and Americans differ sharply in the depth of conversations they feel is appropriate in interpersonal encounters. Among J there is substan-

tially less disclosure of inner experience while among Americans substantially greater disclosure on all topics with all persons".

This variation can also contribute to the negative stereotyping elicited from vagueness versus directness.

When it comes to the use by non-natives of the divergent, culturally specific superstructural sequencing patterns[162], it is vital for cross-cultural communicators to know of their relativity, if they are to avoid being categorized as 'illogical' or, worse, 'stupid' simply because the implicit propositions cannot be taken for granted nor supplied by the listener/reader. For example, one of the characteristic patterns of J oral and written discourse is the dot-type presentation of one item after the other in a highly anecdotal or episodic vein without articulation of the conclusion. Westerners often view such a format as devoid of any particular message, and see the speaker/writer as 'shallow'. The J, in turn, consider the 'forcing' of a conclusion on the listener/reader to be quite unsophisticated and inelegantly simplistic. The diverging interpretability of rhetoric patterns highlights the complexity of cross-cultural interaction. Although fundamentally only forms for presenting and organizing communication, these patterns are falsely evaluated as indicative of their user's abilities and personality traits, thereby assuming a semiotic value.

4.2.4. *The mutual responsibility for miscoding*

In this brief outline of semiotic schism in cross-cultural interaction between members of the J and W speech-communities we have seen that potential miscoding is a joint enterprise: both sides are equally responsible for its occurrence. The study should neither be seen as a list of criticisms nor recipes. It demonstrates how communication, especially the kind that occurs between two radically differing cultural groups, may lead to mutual difficulties in interpretation. As should by now be evident from this section, however, most of communication is mere stylization: verbal politeness strategies, vocal signs of voice quality, kinesic symbols like eye movements and rhetoric patterns for controlling interaction and presenting information are socioculturally established conventions.

Cross-cultural interactants frequently fail to recognize the *conventionality* of the communicative code of the other, instead taking the communicative behaviour as representing what it means in their own native culture. This is the cause of semiotic schism which arises from the interpretive gap between the cognitive models and value systems on which each culture bases its verbal and non-verbal behaviour. The tragedy of semiotic schism is that mere convention and not content should persistently disturb and, on occasions, rupture the already delicate enterprise of cross-cultural communication.

APPENDIX
Background notes on Japanese concepts
of family and marriage

In order to fully appreciate the wedding reception presented in chapter 2 an introductory explanation concerning Japanese family organization and marriage customs is offered to aid the reader with little background knowledge in this area. These notes only provide basic information necessary to understand the content of chapter 2; for further details, see Vogel (1968), Befu (1963), and Fukutake (1967).

In contemporary Japanese society, a variety of family patterns co-exist: nuclear types may be found generally in the cities while in the countryside different forms based usually on the traditional and historically élite family system or *ie* still persist. However, long established town families also tend to model themselves on the *ie* pattern which is a patrilineal stem family or main-lineage family (*honke*) ideally inherited by the eldest son with extended branch families (*bunke*) founded by non-first born sons. In composition these *bunke* may appear as nuclear families but differ from these because they recognize a formal connection with the stem family. The branch family may live with or nearby the stem family and may or may not be involved in its economic or religious activities e.g. if a priest family of a temple or shrine. Frequently today, the *bunke* family lives a great distance away in a city.

The *ie*, therefore, is founded on the principle of a large family into which the component small families are combined and unified under one patriarchal authority. Its primary concern is with the transmission of the family name, property and occupation. Fukutake (1972: 39) points out that the *ie* is "the continuing entity, perpetuated, in principle by patrilineal descent, from ancestors to descendants, an entity of which the family group at any one time is only the current concrete manifestation".

Exactly how to render the concept of *ie* into English has been a problem for anthropologists (cf. Kitaoji 1971: 1036) but this is not our concern here. On the other hand, it is helpful to gain a full awareness of the social and ethical connotations of *ie* as it is continually referred to throughout the reception speeches and an underlying principle of the ethnography. *Ie* (which is also pronounced *-ke* in compounds) includes the physical structure of the domicile, those who live in it — possibly even non-kin employees of the *ie*, the concept of 'family line', for example, as expressed in "The House of (Windsor)" as well as the graveyard where the ancestors are buried, its fields and forest land.

The importance of patrilineage should not be overstressed for bilateral kindred of the wife, sister or mother also form a loose, non-hierarchical network which can sometimes feature very prominently for *ie* members. This bilateral kindred's primary function would seem to be helping to resolve economic problems, celebrating life crises and expressing solidarity. An examination of the guest list at the wedding reception under analysis revealed that non-*ie* relatives also featured prominently at this ritual.

However, as it is the patrilineal *ie* which provides a recognized social structure, a daughter generally joins her husband's *ie* on marriage. Her name is crossed out of her own *ie* and transferred into that of her new husband, so that marriage is viewed less as a union between man and woman and more as the admittance of a woman to a husband's kin group. The nature of this transference is reflected in the Japanese term for such a marriage: *yome-iri* which literally means 'bride-entering'. The insecurity attached to the status of an 'entering bride' and her exploitive reduction to mere child bearer is reflected in various indigenous proverbs such as "parents are irreplaceable but brides can be changed at will", "the womb is something borrowable" and "no child after three years, then divorce".

Since the Meiji period (1868) marriages have traditionally been arranged by *nakōdo* or 'go-betweens whose work task is to ensure that neither of the families' suffer any losses or encroachments of rights as a result of the marriage. Of course, in such arranged marriages family considerations override personal love and affection. However, the wedding under investigation is a 'love match' and not arranged, so that the go-betweens are only ritual figures providing a formal structure to the proceedings. In fact in Japan today the number of 'love marriages' outweighs arranged marriages in urban areas but the opposite is true of the countryside.

FOOTNOTES

1. Neustupný (1984) questions the validity of this estimate of 99% literacy on the basis of two surveys of literacy conducted on subjects aged 14-26 in 1948 and 1955-6 by the Ministry of Education (Monbusho 1961) in which between 20% and 50% of these language users were described as experiencing intense or noticeable problems in the use of the written language. Although only 1% were totally illiterate, as many as 50% to 60% "definitely could be classified as functional illiterates" (1984: 119). Today, no officials acknowledge the existence of illiteracy among the disadvantaged and no new surveys have been conducted since 1956.

2. The Ainu language is not related to Japanese and has been variously identified as linked to Indo-Germanic, Palao-Asiatic, Uralic and Caucasian. If spoken at all, it can only be heard in Hokkaido but it also existed on the mainland one millenium ago. The Ainu were an indigenous but racially and, to some extent culturally, different group from what emerged as 'the Japanese'; they have long been subjected to discrimination and oppression.

3. Among these other residents a number of groups can be identified: educational staff (mainly in English teaching), airline personnel, the temporary foreign business and diplomatic community, foreign students and entertainers.

4. According to the Foreign Ministry, Japanese emigrants overseas and their descendants are estimated at 1,493,800 as of 1980 with 491,000 in Brazil, 45,000 in Peru, 465,000 in the USA including 230,000 in Hawaii, and 30,000 in Canada but, of course, not all of these are proficient in Japanese.

5. Taiwan was annexed to Japan in 1895 and Korea in 1910.

6. For full structural descriptions of Japanese, see Miller (1967), Martin (1975) and Kuno (1973).

7. Japanese employs, in addition to Chinese characters, two syllabaries to phonetically render sounds: *hiragana* which is characterized by its cursive, flowing shapes and *katakana* which is more angular.

8. In the Hepburn system long vowels are represented by overlining with a macron (*ā, ū, ē, ō*) except long *i* is written *ii* e.g. *oniisan*. However, a macron is used over long *i* in loan words and foreign names e.g. bīru. In this work this distinction in Hepburn romanization is not maintained and a long *ī* will be used throughout for the sake of regularity. For a guide to the pronunciation of Japanese (cf. Clarke and Hamamura (1981: 4-11) who provide a simple introduction for English speakers). In the Tokyo dialect, the velar phonemes are /k,g,n/; fricatives: /s,z,c,ʃ,t,tʃ,ʒ,dʒ,h,ɸ/; dentals: /t,d/ and a vibrationless, tongue-tip alveolar flap: /ɾ/; bilabials: /p,b,m,w/; palatal semivocalic: /j/; vowels: /a,i,e,o,u/ (*u* is unrounded and together with *i* often devoiced after voiceless consonants); alveo-palatal /n/ and syllabic nasal /N/ and glottal stop. There are also geminate consonants e.g. /kk, pp, ss, tt/ (cf. Sonoda 1975: 81-123).

9. Cf. Teeter (1973: 506-507): "With honorable exceptions, linguists do not study Japanese linguistics, foreign language specialists do not study 'linguistics' and scholars in Japanese language pay no attention either to linguistics or foreign languages ... The result of this ... is that there are

large amounts of magnificently controlled data in many areas, but few attempts to connect one set of data with another, and little interest in the partly related task of stepping back and viewing the whole from a more abstract point of view".

10. In their preoccupation with the proper interpretation of classical texts, the national language scholars could not circumvent the social context of their production and often deal with sociolinguistic aspects such as women's language, court language, historical regional varieties, religious language, orthographic styles differing according to user's social background as well as text type, and professional varieties such as those of monks, samurai, merchants, prostitutes, craftsmen and fisherfolk.

11. For a summary in English of the findings of some of the surveys of the National Language Research Institute (cf. Grootaers 1982 and Nomoto 1975).

12. Japanese scholars group various linguistic phenomena under honorifics (*keigo*): terms of address and reference cf. 2.2., honorific noun prefixes, routine formulae in which honorifics have become petrified as well as adjectival and verbal honorifics.

13. Here is an example of this subject honorification: 'X reads' expressed in the plainest form (which is not stylistically or socially neutral but can carry intimate or rude connotations depending on the context) is *X ga yomu* (the *ga* is a subject marking particle). If one wishes to exalt X, the verb form changes into the honorific infinitive *yomi* which is encapsulated between the prefix *o-* (or *go-* if it is a Chinese loan) and another verbal construction such as *ni naru* to produce *X ga o-yomi ni naru*. An increasingly popular construction of these exalting referent honorifics is to convert the verb into the passive by adding *(r)are* to the verb stem e.g. *X ga yomareru*.

14. Taking the same example as in note 13 above, 'X (humbly) reads' after object honorification becomes *X ga o-yomi itasu*.

15. Polite addressee honorifics are marked with the presence of morpheme *-masu* e.g. *X ga yomi-masu* 'X reads' and exalting addressee honorifics characterized by the morphemes *gozaru* + masu e.g. *X ga yomu no de gozai+masu* 'X reads'; in the last case, the pleonastic verbosity is self-evident.

16. E.g. *X ga o-yomi itashi-masu* 'X reads' humbles X but respects the addressee.

17. Cf. Nakane (1974: 128-129); "Japanese behave politely when involved with people of the first or second category, but different with strangers ... even to the extent that they may be very rude". Cf. also Peng (1974) who provides an interesting discussion of how the Japanese problem of relating to non-Japanese (the third category in Nakane's classification) is reflected in their lack of polite speech and unwillingness to use Japanese even where the non-native can handle the language fluently.

18. Cf. Shohara (1952: 33): "It is not to be assumed that honorific expressions merely indicate social status. On the contrary, the correct usage of honorific terms serves to indicate the respect of the user for the commendable personal qualities and attainments of the person addressed, such as social responsibility, knowledge, culture etc. It also indicates the cultural status of the speaker".

19. Hinds (1975) carries out a survey which shows that the form for 'he' *kare* is used more by females to refer to male friends but not used to refer to family members of social superiors or people in the public sphere and that its extensive use is considered improper.

20. According to Ishikawa et al. (1981) *fictives* refer to the use of kin terms even though interactants are not blood relatives cf. the use by English children e.g. 'uncle' and 'auntie' to adults who are not related to them. In Japanese, however, such fictives may include 'grandmother', 'grand-

father', 'elder sister' and 'elder brother' as well as 'aunt' and 'uncle' and adults also employ them.

21. Thus, in Japanese, children in a family may call their father *otōsan*, but if old enough, they call their father *chichi* to an outsider.

22. These lexemes corresponding to the English verb 'give' in meaning are *ageru*, *sashiageru*, *yaru*, *kudasaru* and *kureru*.

23. Cf. Miller (1977: 74): "The use of term Okinawa dialect ... is ... semantic slanting of the issues involved. By any usual linguistic definition and terminology, Okinawan is a language geneticaly related to home-island Japanese to be sure, but by no possible stretch of linguistic usage to be considered one of its dialects".

24. The Okinawan kingdom was annexed to the fief of the Satsuma clan in 1609 after being conquered by the clan's lord, Shimazu Iehisa. However, no Japanese emigrants from Satsuma were sent to live there as the islands were secretly used for illegal foreign contacts. It was not until 1879 that Okinawa became a Japanese prefecture during the Meiji Restoration.

25. However, before the 9th century there also exist a few texts in the Japanese language represented in special (phonetic and semantic) orthograhic systems based on Chinese characters such as *manyōgana* and *semmyō-gaki*; such texts include poetry (*Manyōshū*), indigenous ritual prayers (*norito*) and pre-8th century imperial edicts (*semmyō*).

26. Strongly Chinese-influenced written styles include *wakankonkō-bun* (a mixed, Sino-Japanese style), *sōrō-bun* (formal letter style) and *futsū-bun* (the commercial style of the later 19th century).

27. Sexual differentiation is reflected in many extra-linguistic areas, e.g. eating utensils and food types, order of eating (cf. Loveday and Chiba, 1985), Buddhist rosary beads and sleeping posture to name but a few.

28. E.g. *sugoi* 'terrific' > *sugē*; *umai* 'delicious' > *umē*.

29. Sentence final particles that are associated with females include *yo* (emphasizer), *kashira* (= I wonder), *ne* (cf. tag question in English), *wa* (softener), *koto/no* (nominalizer, = case, matter);

30. Male associated particles are *kanā* (= I wonder), *zo/ze* (ends commands and assertions) and *na* (tag).

31. Particularly, the presence of members of the opposite sex.

32. Sexually neutral is a very difficult style to define because it is contextually determined. If a man uses polite forms, that will neutralize his more typically plain style and for a woman vice versa.

33. Ide (1982: 380) observes that although certain lexemes are exclusively used by women and children and would be interpreted as effeminate if used by men, if the latter are "engaged in professions that deal with women and children — such as beauticians, pediatricians and salesmen", they may use them "in order to show empathy toward the addressee".

34. Cf. Helfrich (1979: 88/63). Dynamic age markers are those "markers in speech which reflect the state of the communicative ability of the speaker as related to his age" and which "can be used by the individual according to specific interaction situations" and "are not interpretable without reference to a particular interaction situation". They contrast with static markers of age "with which the individual is endowed as a function of his age".

35. For example, the loan for 'live' was considered as Japanese only by 16 out of 100 informants (aged in their 50's and in authoritative positions) in contrast to 79 out of 104 university students who accepted it as Japanese.

36. For a phonological account, see Tatsuki (1982).

37. Helfrich (1979: 63): "The speech behaviour of a person not only conveys information about his or her own age (sender markers) but also about the listener or the receiver of the verbal message (receiver markers)".

38. Interestingly enough, as Brown and Levinson (1979: 299) point out, only large groups reveal any "deep discontinuities in a number of aspects of communicative competence ... the linguistic discontinuities exist because there are independent bodies of norms governing the use of speech in each such unit, maintained by the kind of internal social network that can sustain such linguistic subcultures".

39. The poll was conducted by the Prime Minister's Office (August, 1985) and covered 10,000 men and women.

40. This refers to the speech-styles of organized gangsters (*yakuza*), juvenile delinquents and prison inmates.

41. Of course, it is not only Japanese linguists who are responsible for this ideology but they seem to be the principal agents of dissemination cf. "Many of the authors of this material are university professors, while others, including a number of the most successful and most important makers of the myth of Nihongo, are employees of government-supported research institutes and similar organizations particularly concerned with the professional study and cultivation of the Japanese language" (Miller 1982: 12).

42. This spiritual energy is known as *koto-dama*.

43. Japan recognizes itself as a 'society of the written word' (*moji-bunka*). The low emphasis placed on teaching oral competence in L2 English, for example, is a reflection of this deprecation of spoken language.

44. Shibata (1985: 87) lists certain tabooed terms for despised professions such as stray-dog catchers, farm labourers and public entertainers as well as socially discriminated groups such as the physically handicapped and the outcast community originally associated with animal slaying and tanning.

45. Cf. Miller (1977: 74): "Japan's linguistic homogeneity, like any other kind of overriding social uniformity, will be bought at the price of stamping out, or at least driving underground, all non-conformist patterns, whether they are the local non-standard dialects of the home islands or independent linguistic entities as the Okinawan language".

46. Cf. in translation: "To say nothing is a flower"; "Mouths are to eat with, not to speak with", "Close your mouth and open your eyes", "Born mouth first, he perishes by his mouth"; "If there are many words, there will be much shame"

47. "Honey in his mouth, a sword in his belly"; "people who praise things, don't buy them"; "Even a lie can be expedient".

48. 'Language planning' constitutes a subfield of sociolinguistics and has already a stock of reference works (cf. Fishman 1974, Rubin et al. 1977, and Cobarrubias and Fishman 1983).

49. The first language planning body was the Kokugo Chōsa Inkai (Commission for the Investigation of the National Language) set up in 1900.

50. These were generally leading intellectual and literary figures of the Meiji era such as Mori Arinori (Education Minister) who argued for the replacement of Japanese by English, Fukuzawa

Yukichi (founder of Keio University) who pleaded for the reduction of characters and Sakaya Rōri who supported the introduction of an international auxiliary language.

51. This movement, named *gembun'itchi*, was launched in the 1880's and stimulated by the seminal work of that name by Mozume Takami in 1886 and by various progressive politicians who adopted colloquial forms in their writings, followed by the development of a modern genre of realism led by writers such as Futabatei Shimei (whose novel "Ukigumo" was the first to approximate the spoken language), culminating in the founding in 1900 of the Society of the Unification of Speech and Writing (*Gembun'itchi-kai*). This style was already taken into account by some primary school texts of 1904 (cf. Lewin 1981: 1179). It entered the press in the 1920's and after 1946 became the official medium. Now, at the end of the 20th century, most written norms follow this literary-spoken variety, although there still remain vestiges of the earlier diglossic High variety in legal and religious styles as well as certain academic writing (cf. Neustupný 1974: 36).

52. The advocates of the romanization of Japanese also began to appear in the 1800's. *Rōmaji-kai* (Society for Roman Script) was founded in 1884, subsequently the *Rōmaji-hirome-kai* (1905) and later *Nippon-Rōmaji-kai* (1921) The first suggestions for romanization were based on the system of the American missionary, J.C. Hepburn, but later Japanese scholars modified this to produce a different version of romanized Japanese which was adopted as the official roman orthography in 1937 by order of the Cabinet and used inside Japan until 1945 when the Hepburn system, favoured by the Americans, once again came to the fore (cf. Lewin 1981).

53. Maejima Hisoka is considered a pioneer of this movement with his early proposal to the last Shogun in 1866 for the replacement of Chinese characters by the sole use of syllabic signs in order to modernize the country by means of easy access to literacy. It is important to remember here that in the history of Japanese literature various respected works had been previously composed only in syllabic orthograhy. A number of societies for the sole employment of the syllabaries (either *katakana* or *hiragana*) were subsequently founded and special newspapers using only these forms published. The central organization was the *Kana no kai*, set up in 1883, which initially had enough influence to effect the style of elementary school texts but later lost its support due to the development and spread of a new literary-spoken language mentioned in note 51 (cf. Lewin 1981).

54. According to Lewin (1979), this urban variety of Meiji Tokyo from which the standard emerged was based on the speech of Yamanote (west of Sumida and stopping at the Imperial Palace) which was a growing residential area of the upper classes, also housing many immigrants from the provinces. This variety was characterized by its openness towards European loans. However, Konrad (1977) points out that features of this variety were already observable in the second half of the 16th century when the contemporary phonetic system was developed, while grammatical features go back as far as the 14th century. It was diffused during the 18th and 19th centuries throughout the country with the publishing of an enormous urban literature using the vernacular.

55. In fact, the Occupation Authorities wanted a complete shift to the sole use of roman script but this was resisted and instead less extreme reforms were carried through. It is clear that the liberal educationalists only had their reforms implemented because of Japan's defeat and the capitulation of the ultraconservatives.

56. Officially created bodies such as the *Rinji-Kokugo-Chōsa-īnkai* (Special Commission for the Investigation of the National Language, 1921-1934) and the *Kokugo-Shingikai* (National Language Council, 1934-1945, 1949- today) provided much of the research for Japanese language and reforms.

57. Cf. note 1.

58. Post-war reforms also tried to regulate honorific usage: in 1957 the Education Ministry issued a document entitled "The honorific language from now on", proposing various guidelines above all for the domains of the media and education (cf. Miller 1967: 285-287). The idea was that language behaviour should accord with the spirit of an egalitarian society, e.g. "The exalted (super-polite) level is an exaggerated type of expression which is not to be encouraged in the future and will gradually drop from usage" (idem).

59. Cf. Miller (1967: 133): "In 1927 the major Tokyo newspapers kept in stock printing type for between 7,500 and 8,000 different Chinese characters, and it was estimated at that time that an 'educated reader' would be 'familiar' with about 5,000 characters".

60. Cf. Miller's (1971: 610) translation of the introduction to Ekoyama Tsuneaki's *Keigohō* (1943): "Now that the construction of Greater East Asia has become the most pressing task of the day for us, it is only to be expected that the Japanese language should present itself as a much debated issue … The permeation of the Japanese language throughout the co-prosperity sphere will require extraordinary exertion and patience".

61. These statements were published in "The Daily Yomiuri", 10 August 1985, p.5., reporting on a round table discussion on the theme of "The Japanese Language in the World" held in Tokyo.

62. According to an article, "Japanese in the World Today", published in "The Daily Yomiuri", 8 and 9 August 1985, p.5. The number of foreign studens in 1984 was only 16,900 according to figures from the Justice Ministry.

63. Due to civil war in China and power struggles at the Japanese court.

64. Cf. Note 2.

65. Many were massacred during the conquest of the northern island of Hokkaido during the 18th and 19th centuries.

66. Significantly, the word for 'temple' (*tera*) is a Korean loan, reflecting the important contribution played by Korean architects in early Japan.

67. Such non-standard Koreanisms include *chongā* 'bachelor', *kīsan* 'geisha' and *pacchi* 'under-pants'. Cf. also 1.3.2.3. and the use of Korean loans in contemporary, university in-group style.

68. Among these Portuguese and Spanish loans still in currency are *pan* 'bread', *tempura* 'batter fries', *kasutera* 'sponge cake', *tabako* 'tobacco', *kirishitan* 'Christian', *shabon* 'soap', *jiban* 'under-shirt', *kappa* 'raincoat' and *rasha* 'wollen cloth'.

69. Examples of Dutch loans include *garasu* 'glass', *kōhi* 'coffee', *bīru* 'beer' *mesu* 'scalpel', *renzu* 'lens' and *arukōru* 'alcohol'.

70. This has often been referred to as 'Japlish' cf. Pierce (1971).

71. Cf. note 35.

72. Gendai-yōgo-no-kiso-shiki, 1977.

73. Cf. Morimoto (1978: 601-602).

74. Cf. Sanches (1977a and 1977b).

75. *Nativization* refers to the change in orientation from external to internal norms. It involves processes of adaption and innovation on any linguistic level which are often the result of a non-native competence and a different socio-cultural environment from the original English context (cf. Kachru 1982a and Richards 1982).

76. The distinction between *code-switching* and *code-mixing* is far from settled but Kachru (1978) differentiates between these two terms in that linguistic units in code-switching are transferred to develop a new restricted code, leading to the emergence of a stabilized variety. Additionally, in code-mixing the transferred elements have reached a stage of considerable integration and community recognition as a particular speech-style.

77. The underlined words have been represented in their English forms for easy recognition. In the original and appearing on a department store leaflet these loans appeared in *katakana*. However, increasingly English words are written in the original roman script while inserted into Japanese orthography e.g. Dynamic な design で tropicalmood 溢れるや …

78. Cf. Sonoda (1975) for a phonological and syntactic study and Miura (1979) for lexico-semantic aspects.

79. Particularly male academic speech.

80. For internal consumption.

81. Loans derived from *informer*, *pawn shop* and *gang* are part of Japanese criminal argot.

82. 'Japanese-based' here means that either the lexicon or the phonology/syntax of the pidgin principally derive from Japanese.

83. Miller (1967: 265) provides a sample text of this 19th century trade pidgin.

84. Cf. Daniels (1948).

85. Cf. note 4 for statistics.

86. For a general, non-linguistic discussion of the social situation of Japanese Brazilians, see Saito (1984).

87. According to the Japanese Foreign Ministry.

88. In fact, Japanese-American family income and male high school graduates now exceed those of whites (Source: Population Reference Bureau Inc. USA, 1985)

89. These are social problems of integration; they are often rejected and ridiculed by classmates.

90. As opposed to Western *horizontal* politeness; cf. Coulmas (1981a, 1981b) on how Japanese routine formulae define interaction stages and social relations.

91. E.g. 'rice plant' (*ine*), 'rice grain' (*kome*), 'cooked rice' (*gohan*) and 'pound, steamed rice' (*mochi*).

92. The sociolinguistic consideration of such special cultural texts should include fossilized oral forms such as Noh theatre, oral narratives such as folktales and religious styles such as chanting routines and Zen questions (*mondō*).

93. E.g. the conferring of a Buddhist death name (the family name changes to *shaku*) or the conferring of a name on joining a Buddhist group (*hōmyō*).

94. This naming symbolism also involves linguistic associations and re-interpretations e.g. seaweed is used to decorate New Year fare because the word for 'seaweed' (*kombu*) is associated with the verb signifying 'to be joyous' (*yoro-kobu*) (cf. Loveday and Chiba 1985).

95. 'Ceremonial go-between' is my coinage to distinguish this role from that of a real go-between or *nakōdo* who arranges marriages. The marriage of the couple at this reception has not been arranged but is the result of their independent choice. Traditionally, the role of go-betweens was to ensure that the rights of each family were safeguarded.

96. Originally, the purpose of the reception, which only dates back to Meiji times (from 1868), was to seek the approbation of the groom's relatives as well as that of the surrounding community of the groom's family. "It included a number of steps that the bride took to insure her acceptance into her new village" (Yanagida 1957: 165). It should be noted that a basic pattern of rural patrilocal marriages in earlier times was for the bride to be collected by a groom's relation from her outlying village and greeted at the gate of the groom's village and finally led to the groom's house, where a celebration would take place with the groom's relatives. This celebration constituted the wedding and during the feasting the bride and groom would ritually eat out of one dish and, in later times, following the fashion of the warrior nobility, drink nine times together. After the celebration, the bride would be presented to the groom's fellow-villagers and friends to whom she distributed gifts and the couple would visit the bride's parents who did not attend the wedding celebration (cf. Segawa 1957 and Yanagida and Omachi 1937). Thus, originally, the reception and the marriage ceremony-contract took place simultaneously. This explains why the first section of this reception is termed 'announcement ceremony' *hirōshiki* and why it follows immediately upon the wedding sipping. It was not until the late 19th century that restaurants became fashionable settings for the reception and that work associates were invited (Yanagida 1957: 165). Until quite recently, only the go-betweens made speeches presenting the couple but today various acquaintances introduce the couple to the guests cf. the reception under discussion.

97. On marriage, a bride's name is crossed out of her own family's record in the local register and entered under her new husband's family line. The nature of this transference is reflected in the Japanese term for such a mariage: *yome-iri*, which literally means 'bride entering'. The insecurity and inferiority attached to the status of an entering bride is reflected also in the proverb "parents are irreplaceable but brides can be changed at will" as well as in the fact that it was not uncommon up to the end of the Second World War that a bride was 'returned' to her original household for any reason determined by her in-laws, with not bearing children the most typical.

98. The bridge in the reception under discussion changes her attire three times during the proceedings- from traditional wedding ceremony kimono to bridal komono to Western-style dress and hat; the groom changes from traditional pleated men's skirt to a white Western suit.

99. The groom's father chose speech-givers solely from his pottery manufacturing associates while the bride's father asked two former Mitsubishi superiors to speak, his cousing serving as go-between.

100. For Freud (1966: 268-83) "rituals" are the everyday acts which have become obsessively repeated ceremonies e.g. Lady Macbeth's hand washing.

101. From ancient times there have been initiation rites marking entry into adult status in Japan. In certain rural districts it was customary to mark the attainment of manhood with the presentation of a loin cloth and the performance of a feat of endurance upon the accomplishment of which the initiated was integrated into the village labour system and permitted to select a wife. At this point, his new social status was recognized with a special name-changing ceremony that replaced his childhood name with an adult one (Wakamori 1963: 234). Japanese philologists relate the word *shinrō* 'groom' with a person who passed an examination to enter the Japanese court bureaucracy. From all this it is clear that the contemporary Japanese notion of being a groom is fundamentally associated with rites de passage both linguistically (in its literal meaning of 'new man') and sociohistorically (in the marital/sexual rights acquired on maturation).

102. "Metacommunications range from quotations, 'I said that I saw the cat' through suprasegmental metalinguistic devices indicating a proper reading of an utterance, 'Oh yeah, that's real pretty' (read: negative truth value) to the elaborate rituals of religious and artistic domains. They

all have in common the feature of referencing some aspect of the communication system —
whether an utterance previously spoken, an element in the code or the major patterns of the grammar of interpersonal relations in the society" (Sanches 1975: 163).

103. I.e. not in Austin's sense (1962); the Hymesian notion of a speech act is the individual component of a speech event.

104. Formulistic incompetence by natives may be interpreted not only as lack of politeness but
also as incomplete socialization. In an analysis of a performance of Japanese comic narrative art
(rakugo), Sanches (1975: 278) describes one instance where the central character of the story
employs the wrong closing formula. He selects *sayonara* for leaving his own place of residence
when the appropriate formula is *itte mairimasu* lit. 'I'm going and coming back'. The error pro-
vokes ridicule and laughter in the audience but points to the social complexity and necessity of formulism. Another socio-evaluative aspect of formulism is how they serve as status definers e.g. 'Hi'
versus 'Good morning'.

105. Cf. Miller (1967: 284-285).

106.   *Etsuko-san   wa shōgakko o kono Yawata no chi   de
          ukeraremashite*
          BRIDE'S NAME primary school this NAME   of area in
          received (PASSIVE +
          ADDRESSEE HONORIFIC)

107. Role terms refer to a variety of address and reference which refer to the designation of persons in terms of their social qualifications, qualities and categories as opposed to their individual
or personal characteristics which is a general sociolinguistic pattern in Japanese e.g. *denkiya-san*
'Mr Electrician', *eigyō buchō* 'Head of the business affairs division', *sensei* 'teacher', *o-kyaku-san*
'customer'.

108. Cf. 2.1. Referent honorifics are a way of showing politeness to a person or other people,
belongings, actions etc. which are related to that person when any of these feature as a subject or
object of a sentence (cf. Comrie 1976 and Harada 1975).

109. Of a more specialized nature, there are also the verbs *ataeru* and *tamawaru* which are both
employed to emphatically elevate givers.

110. From a prescriptive viewpoint, *sashiageru* should only be used when the giver is in the
speaker's group or the speaker himself. However, Kuno (1973: 129) notes "that there are no better
ways of expressing the meaning" of sentence (1). "A use of *ageru* in the place of *sashiageru* in such
a context would strike us as showing a lack of due respect for the teacher".

111. Sentences (7)c and (7)d are both object honorifics (cf. Harada 1975).

112. The choice here, as between *sashiageru* and *ageru* depends on the degree of politeness
required for the donor. There are no sex-linked constraints on the use of *kureru* as in the case with
yaru.

113. This problem is related to the question of 'deictic triangulation' where the addressee's
relationship towards the speaker and referent has a bearing on the form to be selected. Levinson
(1977: 38) finds it less cumbersome to assume that "each form encodes a certain basic relationship
between speaker and the referent *only*" so that the other two relationships (speaker-addressee and
referent-addressee) are "derived by inference from the usage of a particular form by a particular
speaker to a particular referent in a particular context" (ibid.).

114. Cf. Fillmore (1971: 224) who states that it is the linguist's task "to identify the symmetric and asymmetric pronoun choices which the language makes available; he can leave it to scholars in other disciplines to describe the social contexts in which each set of choices can occur".

115. The only example I have found so far where the speaker might switch from *kudasaru* to *ageru* for the listeners/addressee's sake and not for focus or presumed intimacy, is when the speaker is a woman addressing her husband and telling him about her father receiving something. Generally, she would use *kudasaru/kureru* to all addressees but her husband to whom *ageru* would be appropriate. The switch from *kudasaru* to *ageru* would probably imply that she no longer associated closely with her father and her first family group. Interestingly, a man might retain here his first family affiliation and use *kudasaru/kureru*.

116. Although 'Mr' sounds formal enough to English speakers to warrant *kudasaru*, in Japanese Tanaka-*san* is the usual form of address for equals as well as superiors unless a role term such as *sensei* or *buchō* is used for the latter (cf. note 107).

117. I.e. where David is the speaker's brother.

118. Harada (1975: 507) admits there are problems in defining social superiority in "a simple, culture independent way". He mentions the fact that if a student were to join the faculty staff at the university he graduated from, he would still treat his former teachers as superiors as far as honorifics go. Harada considers, however, that "the properties ... associated with a person who is referred to through honorifics is not a problem to which a grammatical description is addressed".

119. According to Harada (1975: 515) work on Japanese generative grammar has pointed towards the transformational introduction of case particles like *ga*.

120. HP refers to the honorific prefix *o-*.

121. If the child were related to the speaker, the donatory form would be *kudasaru*, indicating ingroup membership and a high status giver. Of course, a feature such as SBS (socially belonging to the speaker) would also have to be introduced to distinguish between the two sets relating to in- and outgroup receivers: *kureru* versus *yaru*.

122. Following Harada's arguments (1975: 506) *kudasaru* and *sashiageru* are suppletive forms for **o-kure ni naru* and **o-age suru/itasu* i.e. a syntactic phenomenon. But the weakness of such an approach lies in its inability to differentiate on a stylistic or semantic level within a grammar between *o-age itasu* and *sashiageru*, for example.

123. Others include the existential presupposition that the friend and the camera actually existed.

124. Of course, the meaning *give* will not be handled within pragmatics which basically deals with the relations existing between language and context and the rationale of communication. There would have to be some, as yet undeveloped, framework linking aspects of pragmatics to formal semantics and syntax.

125. "The similarity between reports of explicit performatives and reports of sentences whose illocutionary force is covert can be explained by an appeal to the abstract-performative analysis" (Sadock 1974: 44).

126. *You* is left untranslated in sentence (37)b. as it would most probably be avoided in face-to-face interaction.

127. Anthropological studies have shown that the Japanese household clusters around a descent line of males, usually of father and one son as well as a grandfather, if alive, and members of the household are expected to abide by household decisions, generally issued by the male head, who is thus in a position of strong authority.

128. Cf. Barnlund (1975: 104): "The data suggested that Americans are nearly as close to their fathers as their mothers. Among the Japanese the gulf appeared to be wider. Japanese males ranked their fathers lowest in physical contact ... Japanese females ... not only ranked their fathers substantially below all others (in physical contact) but reported only half as much contact with them as with mothers ... The physical isolation of fathers in Japan, thus, appears to parallel their verbal isolation ... the evidence ... would suggest either a much lower or perhaps fearfully high regard for" fathers by Japanese. "Not only do our respondents appear to disclose little of themselves to their fathers through conversation; they communicate equally little of themselves by means of physical contact".

129. Although there do exist a few families where honorifics are employed by children for parents, they are certainly not the majority (ch. ch.1 section 3.2.3.).

130. The term 'politeness' is intended here to apply to what Brown and Levinson (1978: 75) refer to as "negative politeness" which is "characterized by self effacement, formality and restraint", aiming at reducing the face-threatening implications of a speaker's behaviour.

131. Lehiste and Peterson (1961: 425) conclude that "the phonetic quality of the syllabic sound has an influence on the fundamental frequency at which the intonation level is produced. Further, the initial consonant in a consonant-vowel sequence may influence the F_0 appearing in the vowel following the consonant".

132. Cf. chapter 1 section 1.3.2.1.

133. As none of these concern this study, refer to O'Connor and Arnold (1973: 13-30) for definitions.

134. The dialogue used for the investigation was as follows:
    (Role A was played by the informant)
    A: Oh hello, David.
    B: Oh hello! I didn't see you.
    A: I've heard you've moved house ...
    B: Yes, that's right. We're in Bishopton now.
    A: Oh really! That's a lovely little spot, isn't it? We sometimes go to that pub. 'The Applecart' in the square.
    B: Do you? Well, we live just behind there. If you're not doing anything this Sunday, why don't you come round for lunch?
    A: That's very nice of you. Thank you. What time shall we call?
    B: Oh, around twelve. I'm sorry. I have to rush off now. I'm in a dreadful hurry.
    A: Yes, of course.
    B: So, we'll see you on Sunday then ...
    A: Yes, about twelve.
    B: Right. Bye.
    A: Bye.

    A: ā, konnichi wa, Yamada-san desu nē?
    B: ā, konnichi wa. Hisashiburi desu nē.
    A: Hikkoshi shita to kikimashita ga, dochira e?
    B: Kyōto e nē.
    A: Kyōto desu ka? Ii tokoro e hikkosaremashita nē!
       Watashi mo nagaku Kyōto e itta koto ga arimasen ga, ichido itte mitai desu nē.
    B: Watashi no uchi wa Saga ni arimasu. Kondo no nichiyōbi demo uchi e kimasen ka?
    A: Arigatō gozaimasu.

B: Kore wa watashi no denwa bango desu. Eki e tsuitara, denwa shite kuremasenka? Kuruma de mukae ni yukimasu yo. Kyō wa isoide iru no de, shitsurei shimasu. Sayōnara.

B: Sayōnara.

135. Naturally, it is not assumed that this is less reliable or accurate than by technical measurement, since no absolutely reliable method of obtaining exact pitch range readings exists. Professor Abramson (personal communication) has pointed out that speakers of a language "function in production and perception with prosodic features ..." and so "... it must follow that certain kinds of impressionistic auditory analysis are relevant".

136. Crystal (1975: 79) mentions room size and temperature as also significant.

137. Cf. Crystal's remarks (1975: 78): "the fact that different scholars on different occasions can transcribe different voices with relatively little disagreement ... suggests that we do as a matter of course introduce some kind of phonetic consistentizing principle into our analyses".

138. Brown and Levinson (1978: 272) also mention a "sustained falsetto" employed in Tzeltal in ritual situations such as greeting formulae and sometimes over "entire formal interaction". Albert (1972) comments on the use of pitch in the voice training of Burundi boys who have to learn a special "tone of voice and its modulation" (p.77) together with "a suitable elegant vocabulary ... graceful gestures with hand and spear" for deflecting the anger of a superior and when serving as an intermediary between a petitioner and one's feudal superior".

139. 'High' in relation to the Japanese male subjects' performance.

140. No overt reference is made to the individual research areas as such since this would considerably lengthen this section and slow down the presentation.

141. One who aids or joins in the dissension within the system of organization.

142. By psychological imbalance I refer to the existence of complexes vis-à-vis other interactants from different cultural, ethnic or racial groups.

143. It is obvious that the linguistic behaviour in this paper is viewed as closely intertwined with and interdependent upon the sociocultural context in which it is employed (cf. Bauman and Sherzer 1974).

144. As is well known, it is extremely difficult to determine interactional meaning in a straightforward manner since in interaction a mass of diverse signs are produced and their interrelations and semantic priority are still a matter of debate.

145. Interpersonal attribution refers to the processes "by which we come to attribute various dispositions, motives, intentions, abilities and responsibilities to one another — in short, how we come to describe one another in particular ways ... when we make an attribution about another person, therefore, we are essentially trying to interpret or explain his behaviour, and in so doing render our social environment that much more predictable and intelligible" (Eifer 1978: 235-237).

146. Note here the extent to which Japanese culture is directed beyond the self to others in terms of belonging, empathy, dependency and reciprocity.

147. These phrases represent abstract values in Japanese society.

148. The Japanese frequently comment on their difficulty in assessing the age of Caucasians.

149. The seminal work on politeness strategies is that of Brown and Levinson (1978) who develop the categories of negative and positive politeness.

150. "Positive politeness ir orientated towards the positive face of (the) H(earer), the positive self-image that he claims for himself. Positive politeness is approach-based; it 'anoints' the face of the addressee by indicating that in some respects, (the) S(peaker) wants (the) H(earer)'s wants (e.g. by treating him as a member of an ingroup, a friend, a person whose wants and personality traits are known and liked). The potential face threat of an act is minimized in this case by the assurance that in general the S(peaker) wants at least some of (the) H(earer)'s wants; for example, that S considers H to be in important respects 'the same' as he, with ingroup rights and duties and expectations of reciprocity" (Brown and Levinson 1978: 75).

151. This may be because of later historical development of social organizational forms based on an egalitarian, non-feudalistic ethos (cf. Neustupný 1974).

152. 'Interference' is a term belonging to the field of behaviourist psychology and is used here to refer to the negative transfer of L1 features to an L2.

153. The number 20 is taken here for the standard British (English English) Received Pronunciation variety of English.

154. 'Foreigner talk' is the simplified and pidgin-like speech of natives which rarely corresponds to the authentic nature of L2 speech but more to folk notions of how foreigners are expected to speak — and how they should be spoken to (cf. Ferguson 1981 and chapter 1, section 1.4.).

155. Of course, this is relatively speaking. It appears 'loud' to the Westerner.

156. Lip puckering occurs in English-speaking communities in baby-talk expressions such as 'kut-shee kutshee koo'.

157. "In everyday interpersonal relationships, the act of staring at the person to whom one is talking is quite extraordinary and considered to be rude. To be continuously stared at creates displeasure for the Japanese, except among very intimate relations. To look intently at the person to whom one is talking does not, for the Japanese, signify respect. Rather, a tendency to look downward is appreciated even today, especially among females, and is thought to be suggestive of a certain elegance. Thus, there exists a cultural characteristic which causes Japanese to be hypersensitive about 'looking at' and 'being looked at' (Kasahara 1974: 402).

158. Adaptors "are perhaps the most difficult (kinesic signs) to define and involve the most speculation. They are labeled adaptors because they are thought to develop in childhood as adaptive efforts to satisfy needs, perform actions, manage emotions, develop social contacts, or perform a host of other functions. Ekman and Friesen have identified three types of adaptors: self-, object-, and alter-directed ... Alter-adaptors are learned in conjunction with our early experiences with interpersonal relations — giving and taking from another, attacking or protecting, establishing closeness or withdrawing, and the like" (Knapp 1978: 17).

159. It was a mortal offence to smile showing the back teeth when addressing a superior. In all classes, demeanour was severely regulated and this is still evident today.

160. The Japanese stress on the non-personalized use of routine formulae is demonstrated in a questionnaire reported in Loveday (1982b) when I asked Japanese students and English native informants (1) What would you say to someone who saved you from drowning? and (2) What would you say to someone who gave you a birthday present? The majority of Japanese used the same formula for both (1) and (2) while many of the English informants responded to (1) with answers such as "I don't know how to thank you" and "Thanks. God. What can I say?" and one even wrote: "Really, I don't know what to say. 'Thankyou' seems so pathetic, seeing as you've saved my life, but all I can say is 'thanks' and I really mean it". The English responses clearly indi-

cate that the use of the polite formula was considered to be insufficient expression of the gratitude for having one's life saved. Additionally, in contrast to the unified response from the Japanese students to (2), the English informants gave many individualized answers for (2) such as "it was very thoughtful of you to remember my birthday" and "Gosh. That's marvellous. Thank you very much" etc. thereby illustrating their need for a more personalized reaction.

161. Cf. Ogasawara (1972: 14) who writes: "komakaku hakkiri yū hito ga ireba, sono hito wa okashi na hito de aru to yū koto ni mo naru" (... if someone speaks in a clear, detailed manner he may be considered strange).

162. Superstructural sequencing is a rhetoric pattern which ensures textual cohesion and coherence through linguistic means such as repetition, substitution and deletion among others. The sequencing follows certain principles or purposes that belong to generally unconscious social knowledge. "In order to make sense of acceptable paragraphs, essays, monologues, etc. the listener-interpreter has to make connections between the propositions in each statement. These connections are generally not expressed since the speaker (writer assumes them to be accessible). However, the connections are contextually and culturally determined. They are related in part to the pragmatic notion of presupposition. Without these implicit presupposed connections, the text or discourse would not be intelligible" (Loveday 1983: 182)

REFERENCES

Abe, Isamu
    1955   "Intonation". Reprinted in D. Bolinger (ed.) 1972, *Intonation*. Harmondsworth: Penguin, 337-347.

Abercrombie, David
    1967   *Elements of general phonetics*. Edinburgh: Edinburgh University Press.

Adams, J.B.
    1957   "Culture and conflict in an Egyptian village". *American Anthropologist* 59.225-235.

Albert, Ethel M.
    1972   "Culture patterning of speech behaviour in Burundi". In John Gumperz and Dell Hymes (ed.) 1972, 72-105.

Algeo, John T.
    1960   "Korean Bamboo English". *American Speech* 35.117-123.

Asuncion-Landé, Nobleza and Emy M. Pascasio
    1979   "Language maintenance and code-switching among Filipino bilingual speakers". In F.W. Mackey and Jacob Ornstein (eds.) 1979, 211-229.

Austin, John L.
    1962   *How to do things with words*. Oxford: Oxford University Press.

Barnlund, Dean C.
    1975   *Public and private self in Japan and the United States*. Tokyo: Simul Press.

Bates, Elizabeth and L. Benigni
    1975   "Rules of address in Italy: a sociological survey". *Language in Society* 4.271-288.

Bauman, Richard and Joel Sherzer (eds.)
    1974   *Explorations in ethnography of speaking*. Cambridge: Cambridge University Press.

Befu, Harumi
    1963   "Patrilineal descent and personal kindred in Japan". *American Anthropologist* 65.1328-1341.

Befu, Harumi and Edward Norbeck
    1958   "Japanese usages of terms of relationship". *Southwestern Journal of Anthropology* 14.66-86.

Beltramo, Anthony F.
    1981   "Profile of a state: Montana". In C.A. Ferguson and S.B. Heath (eds.) 1981, 339-380.

Benedict, Ruth
   1946   *The chrysanthemum and the sword*. London: Routledge and Kegan Paul.

Bolitho, M. Anne
   1976   "Communicative networks of Japanese women in Melbourne". In Michael Clyne
            (ed.) 1976, *Australia talks*. (Pacific Linguistics Series D-No.23). Dept. of Linguistics,
            Research School of Pacific Studies: Australian National University, 103-115.

Braunroth, M., G. Seyfert, K. Siegel, and F. Vahle
   1975   *Ansätze und Aufgaben der linguistischen Pragmatik*. Frankfurt/M: Athenäum.

Brend, R.M.
   1972   "Male-female intonation patterns in American English". In *Proceedings of the 9th
            International Congress of Phonetic Sciences*. The Hague: Mouton, 866-870.

Brown, Penelope and Stephen Levinson
   1978   "Universals in language usage: politeness phenomena". In Esther N. Goody (ed.)
            1978, *Questions and Politeness*. Cambridge: Cambridge University Press, 56-310.

   1979   Social structure, groups and interaction. In Klaus R. Scherer and H. Giles (eds.)
            1979, 291-341.

Brown, Penelope and Colin Fraser
   1979   "Speech as a marker of situation". In Klaus R. Scherer and Howard Giles (eds.) 1979,
            33-62.

Brown, R. and A. Gilman
   1972   "The pronouns of power and solidarity". In Pier Paulo Giglioli (ed.) 1972, *Language
            and social context*. Harmondsworth: Penguin, 252-282.

Cammack, Floyd M. and Hildebert van Buren
   1967   "Paralanguage across cultures". *English Language Education Council Bulletin*
            (Tokyo) 22.7-10.

Chomsky, Noam and M. Halle
   1968   *The sound pattern of English*. New York: Harper and Row.

Clancy, Patricia M.
   1982   "Written and spoken style in Japanese narratives". In Deborah Tannen (ed.) 1982,
            Spoken and written language. Norwood, New Jersey: Ablex, 55-76.

Clarke, H.D.B. and Hamamura Motoko
   1981   *Colloquial Japanese*. London: Routledge and Kegan Paul.

Cobarrubias, Juan and Joshua A. Fishman (eds.)
   1983   *Progress in language planning*. Berlin: Mouton.

Cohen, L.J.
   1970   "Speech acts". (unpublished paper)

Cole, Peter (ed.)
   1978   *Syntax and semantics 9: Pragmatics*. New York: Academic Press.

Cole, Peter and Jerry Morgan (eds.)
1975   *Syntax and semantics 3: Speech acts*. New York: Academic Press.

Comrie, Bernard
1976   "Linguistic politeness axes". *Pragmatics Microfiche* 1.7.A3.

Condon, John C. and Mitsuko Saito (eds.)
1974   *Intercultural encounters*. Tokyo: Simul Press.

Cooper, M. and N. Yanagihara
1971   "A study of the basal pitch level variations found in the normal speaking voices of males and females". *Journal of Communication Disorders* 3.261-266.

Coulmas, Florian
1979   "Riten des Alltags". In W. van de Weghe and M. van de Velde (eds.) 1979, *Bedeutung, Sprechakte und Texte* Vol.2 Tübingen: Niemeyer, 171-180.

1981   "Poison to your soul: Thanks and apologies contrastively viewed". In F. Coulmas (ed.) 1981, 69-91.

Coulmas, Florian (ed.)
1981   *Conversational routine*. The Hague: Mouton.

Crosby, P. and L. Nyquist
1977   "The female register: An empirical study of Lakoff's hypothesis". *Language in Society* 6.313-321.

Crystal, David
1969   *Prosodic systems and intonation in English*. Cambridge: Cambridge University Press.

1975   *The English tone of voice*. London: Edward Arnold.

Cuceloglu, D.
1967   *A cross-cultural study of communication via facial expressions*. Ph.D. dissertation, University of Illinois.

DAIJITEN.
         Tokyo: Heibonsha. Vol.13/14.

Daniels, F.J.
1948   "The vocabulary of the Japanese ports lingo". *Bulletin of the Society for Oriental Studies* 12.805-823.

Denes, Peter
1959   "A preliminary investigation of certain aspects of intonation". *Language and Speech* 2.106-122.

Denes, Peter and J. Milton-Williams
1962   "Further studies in intonation". *Language and Speech* 5.1-14.

Deva, B.C.
1957   "Psychophysics of speech melody, Part 1". *Zeitschrift für Phonetik und allgemeine Sprachwissenschaft* 10.337-344.

1958   "Psychophysics of speech melody, Part 2". *Zeitschrift für Phonetik und allgemeine Sprachwissenschaft* 11.206-211.

1960   "Psychophysics of speech melody, Part 3 and 4". *Zeitschrift für Phonetik und allgemeine Sprachwissenschaft* 13.8-18;19-27.

De Vos, George A. (ed.)
1973   *Socialization for achievement*. Berkeley: University of California Press.

Dittmar, Norbert
1976   *Sociolinguistics: A critical survey of theory and application*. London: Edward Arnold.

Doi, Takeo
1956   "Japanese language as an expression of Japanese psychology". *Western Speech* 20.90-96.

1973   *The anatomy of dependence*. Tokyo: Kodansha.

Driver, H.E. and W. Driver
1963   *Ethnography and acculturation of the Chichimeca-Jonaz of North-East Mexico*. The Hague: Mouton.

Durkheim, Emile
1972   *Selected Writings*, ed. by A. Giddens. Cambridge: Cambridge University Press.

Edelsky, C.
1979   "Question intonation and sex roles". *Language in Society* 8.15-32.

Eiser, Richard J.
1978   "Interpersonal attributions". In Henri Tajfel and Colin Fraser (eds.) 1978, *Introducing social psychology*. Harmondsworth: Penguin, 235-255.

Ekman, Paul and Wallace V. Friesen
1969   "The repertoire of nonverbal behaviour". *Semiotica* 1.49-98.

Erikson, F. et al.
1973   *Interethnic relations in urban institutional settings*. Rockville: National Institute of Mental Health.

Ervin-Tripp, Susan
1968   "An analysis of the interaction of language, topic and listener". In J.A. Fishman (ed.) 1968, *Readings in the sociology of language*. The Hague: Mouton, 192-211.

1969   "Sociolinguistic rules of address". In John B. Pride and David Holmes (eds.) 1972, 225-240.

Farb, Peter
1973   *Word play: What happens when people talk*. New York: Knopf.

Ferguson, Charles
1981   "'Foreigner talk' as the name of a simplified register". *International Journal of the Sociology of Language* 28.9-18.

Ferguson, Charles A. and Shirley B. Heath (eds.)
  1981   *Language in the USA*. Cambridge: Cambridge University Press.

Fillmore, Charles
  1971   "Towards a theory of deixis". *Working Papers in Linguistics* (Honolulu) 3.4.

  1973   "A grammarian looks to sociolinguistics". *Georgetown University Monographs in Language and Linguistics* 25.273-87.

  1975   *Santa Cruz lectures on deixis*. Bloomington: Indiana University Linguistics Club.

Firth, Raymond
  1972   "Verbal and bodily rituals of greeting and parting". In J.S. La Fontaine (ed.) 1972, *The interpretation of ritual*. London: Tavistock.

Fischer, John L.
  1970   "Linguistic socialization: Japan and the United States". In: R. Hill and R. König (eds.) 1970, *Families in East and West*. Paris: Mouton, 107-119.

Fischer, John L. and Yoshida Teigo
  1968   "The nature of speech according to Japanese proverbs". *Journal of American Folklore* 81.34-43.

Fishman, Joshua A.
  1969   *The sociology of language*. Rowley, Mass.: Newbury House.

  1974   *Advances in language planning*. The Hague: Mouton.

Fitzgerald, D.K.
  1975   "The language of ritual events among the Ga of southern Ghana". In Mary Sanches and Ben Blount (eds.) 1975, 205-234.

Fodor, Janet Dean
  1977   *Semantics: Theories of meaning in generative grammar*. New York: Crowell.

Fraser, Bruce
  1971   "An examination of the performative analysis". Bloomington: Indiana University Linguistics Club.

Fraser, Bruce and William Nolen
  1981   "The association of reference with linguistic form". *International Journal of the Sociology of Language* 27.93-109.

Freud, Sigmund
  1966   *A general introduction to psychoanalysis*. New York: Washington Square Press.

Friedrich, Paul
  1972   "Social context and semantic feature: the Russian pronominal usage". In John J. Gumperz and Dell Hymes (eds.) 1972, 270-300.

Fry, D.B.
  1968   "Prosodic phenomena". In Bertil Malmberg (ed.) 1968, *Manual of phonetics*. Amsterdam: North Holland, 365-410.

Fukutake, Tadashi
    1972   *Japanese rural society*. London: Cornell University Press.

Gazdar, Gerald
    1980   "Pragmatic constraints on linguistic production". In Brian Butterworth (ed.) 1980,
             Language production. London: Academic Press, 49-68.

Gibney, Frank
    1975   *Japan: The fragile superpower*. Tokyo: Tuttle.

Giles, Howard
    1978   "Linguistic differentiation in ethnic groups". In Henri Tajfel (ed.) 1978, *Differentia-
             tion between social groups*. London: Academic Press.

Giles, Howard, Donald Taylor and Richard Bourhis
    1973   "Towards theory of interpersonal accommodation through language: some Canadian
             data". *Language in Society* 2.177-192.

Glissmeyer, Gloria
    1973   "Some characteristics of English in Hawaii". In R.W. Bailey and J.L. Robinson
             (eds.) 1973, *Varieties of present-day English*. London: Macmillan, 190-225.

Goffman, Erving
    1967   *Interaction ritual*. Harmondsworth: Penguin.

Goldstein, Bernice Z. and Kyoko Tamura
    1975   *Japan and America*. Tokyo: Tuttle.

Goodman, J.S.
    1967   "The development of a dialect of English-Japanese pidgin". *Anthropological Linguis-
             tics* 9:6.43-55.

Goody, Jack
    1961   "Religion and ritual: the definition problem". *British Journal of Sociology* 12.143-
             164.

Grewendorf, G.
    1972   "Sprache ohne Kontext: zur Kritik der performativen Analyse". In Dieter Wunder-
             lich (ed.) 1972, 144-182.

Grice, H. Paul
    1975   "Logic and conversation". In Peter Cole and Jerry Morgan (eds.) 1975, 41-58.

Grootaers, Willem A.
    1967   "Japanese dialectology". In T.A. Sebeok (ed.) 1967, *Current trends in linguistics*,
             Vol.2. The Hague: Mouton, 585-607.

    1983   "The Japanese language". In *Kodansha Encyclopedia of Japan*, vol 1. Tokyo:
             Kodansha, 23-29.

Grootaers, Willem A. and Takeshi Shibata
    1982   "Dialectology and sociolinguistics: a general survey". *Lingua* 57.327-355.

Gumperz, John J.
  1964   "Linguistic and social interaction in two communities". *American Anthropologist* 66.137-154.

  1975   "Foreword". In Mary Sanches and Ben Blount (eds.) 1975, 1-10.

Gumperz, John J. and Dell Hymes (eds.)
  1972   *Directions in sociolinguistics*. New York: Holt, Rinehart and Winston.

Haarman, Harald
  1984   "The role of ethnocultural stereotypes and foreign languages in Japanese commercials". *International Journal of the Sociology of Language* 50.101-121.

Haas, Mary
  1944   "Men's and women's speech in Koasati". *Language* 40.142-149.

Hall, Edward T.
  1972   "Silent assumptions in social communication". In John Laver and Sandy Hutcheson (eds.) 1972, 274-288.

Hammitzsch, Horst (ed.)
  1981   *Japan-Handbuch*. Wiesbaden: Franz Steiner.

Harada, S.
  1975   "Honorifics". In M. Shibatani (ed.) 1975, *Syntax and semantics 5: Japanese generative grammar*. New York: Academic Press, 499-570.

Hartmann, Dietrich
  1973   "Begrüssungen und Begrüssungsrituale". *Zeitschrift für germanistische Linguistik* 1.133-162.

Haugen, Einar
  1975   "Pronominal address in Icelandic". *Language in Society* 4.323-339.

Helfrich, Hede
  1979   "Age markers in speech". In K.R. Scherer and H. Giles (eds.) 1979, 63-107.

Henley, Nancy and Barrie Thorne
  1975   "Sex differences in language, speech and nonverbal communication: An annotated bibliography". In B. Thorne and N. Henley (eds.) 1975, 205-305.

Higa, Masanori
  1975   "The use of loanwords in Hawaiian Japanese". In F.C.C. Peng (ed.) 1975, 71-89.

  1979   "Sociolinguistic aspects of word borrowing". *Topics in Culture Learning* 1.75-85.

Hioki, Kōjirō
  1981   "Normen und Werte". In Hammitzch, H. (ed.) 1981, 640-646.

Hinds, John
  1975   "Third person pronouns in Japanese". In F.C. Peng (ed.) 1975, 129-157.

  1976a   "A taxonomy of Japanese discourse types". *Linguistics* 184.45-53.

1976b   *Aspects of Japanese discourse structure*. Tokyo: Kaitakusha.

1979   "Organizational patterns in discourse". In T. Givón (ed.) 1979, *Syntax and semantics 12: Discourse and syntax*. New York: Academic Press, 135-157.

1980   "Japanese expository prose". *Papers in Linguistics* 13.117-158.

1982a.   "Japanese conversational structures". *Lingua* 57.301-326.

1982b   "Case marking in Japanese". *Linguistics* 20.541-557.

1983   "Linguistics and written discourse in English and Japanese: a contrastive study". In R.B. Kaplan et al. (eds.) 1983, *Annual review of applied linguistics*. Rowley, Mass.: Newbury House, 78-84.

Hollien, H., D. Dew and P. Philips
1971   "Phonational frequency ranges of adults". *Journal of Speech and Hearing Research* 14.755-760.

Honna, Nobuyuki
1975   "A note on social structure and linguistic behaviour: a case study of a Japanese community". In F.C. Peng (ed.) 1975, 193-214.

Hrdlickovà, V.
1969   "Japanese professional storytellers". *Genre* 12.179-210.

Hymes, Dell
1971   "On communicative competence". In John B. Pride and David Holmes (eds.) 1972, 269-293.

1972   "Models of the interaction of language and social life". In J. Gumperz and D. Hymes (eds.) 1972, 35-71.

Ide, Sachiko
1982   "Japanese sociolinguistics, politeness and women's language". *Lingua* 57.357-385.

1983   "Two functional aspects of politeness in women's language". In S. Hattori and K. Inoue (eds.) 1983, *Proceedings of the XIIIth International Congress of Linguists*. Tokyo: International Congress of Linguists, 805-808.

Inoue, F.
1979   "Wakamono no keigo kōdō". [Young people's honorific behaviour]. *Gengo* 8:6.38-46.

Irvine, J.T.
1975   *Wolof speech styles and social status*. Unpublished ms. Southwest educational development. lab. Austin, Texas.

Ishikawa, A. et al.
1981   "Address terms in modern Japanese: a sociolinguistic analysis". *Sophia Linguistica* 8/9.120-140.

Ishino, Hiroshi
1983   *Gendai-gairaigo-kō* [Thoughts on contemporary foreign borrowings]. Tokyo: Taishūkan.

Jacobs, Roderick A. and Peter S. Rosenbaum (eds.)
1970   *Readings in English Transformational Grammar.* Waltham, Mass.: Ginn.

Japanese National Language Research Institute (Kokugo Kokuritsu Kenkyūjo)
1955-1975 *The Linguistic Atlas of Japan* (Nihongo Gengo Chizu). Tokyo: Kokugo Kokuritsu Kenkyūjo.

1964   *Gendai Zasshi kyūjū shū no yōji yōgo* [Infant terms in 90 contemporary magazines]. Tokyo: Shūei.

Jorden, H.
1983a   "Feminine language". In *Kodansha Encyclopedia of Japan*, vol.2. Tokyo: Kodansha, 250-251.

1983b   "Masculine language". In *Kodansha Encyclopedia of Japan*, vol.5, Tokyo: Kodansha, 124-125.

Kachru, Braj B.
1982   "Models for non-native Englishes". In B.B. Kachru (ed.) 1982, 31-57.

Kachru, Braj B. (ed.)
1982   *The other tongue — English across cultures.* Urbana: University of Illinois.

Kasahara, Yomishi
1974   "Fear of eye-to-eye confrontation among neurotic patients in Japan". In Takie Sugiyama and William P. Lebra (eds.) 1974, *Japanese culture and behaviour.* Honolulu: East-West Center Press, 396-406.

Katz, Jerrold J. and Janet Dean Fodor
1963   "The structure of a semantic theory". *Language* 39.170-210.

Kawasaki, I.
1970   *Japan unmasked.* Tokyo: Tuttle.

Key, Marie Ritchie
1972   "Linguistic behavior of male and female". *Linguistics* 88.15-31.

1975   *Paralanguage and kinesics.* Metuchen, New Jersey: Scarecrow Press.

Kukuzawa, Sueo
1936   *Shinkō Kokugogaku josetsu* [Introduction to a new approach to national language study]. Tokyo: Bungakusha.

Kishitani, Shoko
1969   "Der japanische Honorativ und seine Verwendung in der Sprache der Gegenwart". In Bruno Lewin (ed.) 1969, *Beiträge zum interpersonalen Bezug im Japanischen.* Wiesbaden: Otto Harrassowitz, 1-17.

Kitaoji, H.
1971   "The structure of the Japanese family". *American Anthropologist* 73.1036-1055.

Klineberg, Otto
1935   *Race differences*. New York: Harper and Row.

Knapp, Mark L.
1978   *Nonverbal communication in human interaction*. New York: Holt, Rinehart and Winston.

Konrad, N.I.
1977   "On the literary language in China and Japan". In P.A. Luelsdorff (ed.) 1977, *Soviet contributions to the sociology of language*. The Hague: Mouton, 31-73.

Kramer, C.
1974   "Women's speech: separate but unequal". In Barrie Thorne and Nancy Henley (eds.) 1975, 43-56.

Kramer, E.
1964   "Elimination of verbal cues in judgements of emotion from voice". *Journal of Abnormal and Social Psychology* 68.390-396.

Kunihiro, Masao
1975   "Indigenous barriers to communication". *Japan Interpreter* 8.96-108.

Kuno, Susumu
1973   *The structure of the Japanese language*. Cambridge, Mass.: MIT Press.

Ladefoged, Peter
1975   *A course in phonetics*. New York: Harcourt Brace Javanovich.

Lakoff, George
1971   "Presuppositions and relative well-formedness". In Danny D. Steinberg and Leon A. Jakobovits (eds.) 1971, *Semantics*. Cambridge: Cambridge University Press, 329-340.

Lakoff, Robin
1972   "Language in context". *Language* 48.907-27.

1975   *Language and women's place*. New York: Harper and Colophon.

Laver, John
1975   *Individual features in voice quality*. Ph.D. thesis, University of Edinburgh.

Laver, John and Sandy Hutcheson (eds.)
1972   *Communication in face-to-face interaction*. Harmondsworth: Penguin.

Laver, John and Peter Trudgill
1979   "Phonetic and linguistic markers in speech". In Klaus R. Scherer and Giles Howard (eds.) 1979, 1-32.

Leach, Edmund R.
1976   *Culture and communication: The logic by which symbols are connected*. Cambridge: Cambridge University Press.

Lebra, Takie Sugiyama
    1976   *Japanese patterns of behavior*. Honolulu: East-West Center Press.

Lehiste, Ilse and G.E. Peterson
    1961   "Some basic considerations in the analysis of intonation". *Journal of the Acoustical Society of America* 33.419-425.

Levinson, Stephen
    1977   *Social deixis in a Tamil village*. Ph.D. thesis, University of California, Berkeley.

    1978   *Pragmatics and social deixis*. (unpublished paper).

Lewin, Bruno
    1979   "Demokratisierungsprozesse in der modernen Sprachentwicklung". In K. Kracht (ed.), *Japan nach 1945*. Wiesbaden: Harrassowitz, 87-101.

    1981   "Sprache". In H. Harrassowitz (ed.) 1981, 1717-1802.

Lewis, D.
    1972   "General semantics". In Donald Davidson and Gilbert Harman (eds.) 1972, *Semantics of natural language*. Dordrecht: Reidel, 69-218.

Lieberman, Philip
    1967   *Intonation, perception and language*. Cambridge, Mass.: MIT Press.

Loveday, Leo
    1981   "Pitch, politeness and sexual role". *Language and Speech* 24.71-89.

    1982a   "Japanese donatory verbs: their implications for linguistic theory". *Studia Linguistica* 36.1.39-63.

    1982b   "Communicative interference: a framework for contrastively analysing L2 communicative competence exemplified with the linguistic behaviour of Japanese performing in English". *International Review of Applied Linguistics* 20:2.1-16.

    1982c   *The sociolinguistics of learning and using a non-native language*. Oxford: Pergamon Press.

    1983   "Rhetoric patterns in conflict: the sociocultural relativity of discourse-organizing processes". *Journal of Pragmatics* 7.169-190.

    1984   "The ecology of designatory markers". In W. Enninger and M. Lilith (eds.) 1984, *Studies in language ecology*. Wiesbaden: Franz Steiner, 83-93.

    1985   "At cross-purposes: semiotic schism in Japanese-Western interaction". In R.J. Brunt and W. Enninger (eds.) 1985, *Interdisciplinary perspectives at cross-cultural communication*. (= Aachener Studien zur Semiotik und Kommunikationsforschung, Bd.2.) Aachen: Rader, 31-63.

Loveday, Leo and Satomi Chiba
    1985   "Partaking with the divine and symbolizing the societal: the semiotics of Japanese food and drink". *Semiotica* 56.1/2,115-131.

Luchsinger, R. and G. Arnold
  1965   *Voice-speech-language*. Belmont: Wadsworth.

Mackey, William Francis and Jacob Ornstein (eds.)
  1979   Sociolinguistic studies in language contact. The Hague: Mouton.

Makino, Seiichi
  1970   "Two proposals about Japanese polite expressions". In Jerrold Sadock and A. Vanek
          (eds.) 1970, *Studies presented to R.B. Lees by his students*. Edmonton, Alberta: Lin-
          guistic Research Inc., 163-187.

Malinowski, Bronislaw
  1961   *Argonauts of the Western Pacific*. New York: Dutton.

Martin, Samuel E.
  1954   *Essential Japanese*. Tokyo: Charles Tuttle.

  1964   "Speech levels in Japan and Korea". In D. Hymes (ed.) 1964, *Language in culture and
          society*. New York: Harper and Row, 407-415.

  1967   "On the accent of Japanese adjectives". *Language* 43.246-277.

  1975   *A reference grammar of Japanese*. New Haven: Yale University Press.

Mehrotra, Raja Ram (ed.)
  1985   *Sociolinguistic surveys in South, East, and Southeast Asia*. (= International Journal of
          the Sociology of Language, No.55.) Berlin: Mouton.

Miller, Andrew Roy
  1967   *The Japanese language*. Chicago: University of Chicago Press.

  1971   "Levels of speech (keigo) and the Japanese linguistic response to modernization". In
          D.H. Shively (ed.) 1971, *Tradition and modernization in Japanese culture*. Princeton:
          Princeton University Press, 601-665.

  1977   *The Japanese language in contemporary Japan*. (AEI — Hoover Policy Studies 22).
          Washington D.C.: American Enterprise Institute for Public Policy Research.

  1982   *Japan's modern myth: The language and beyond*. New York: Weatherhill.

Mio, I.
  1958   *Hanashi-kotoba no bumpō*. Tokyo: Hōsei-Daigaku-Shuppan-Kyoku.

Mizutani, Osamu
  1981   Japanese: the spoken language in Japanese lige. Tokyo: Japan Times.

Morgan, Jerry L.
  1975   "Some interactions of syntax and pragmatics". In Peter and Jerry L. Morgan (eds.)
          1978, 289-303.

  1978   "Two types of convention in indirect speech acts". In Peter Cole (ed.) 1978, 261-280.

Morito, Yoshihisa
  1978   "Japanese English". In Ikuo Koike et al. (eds.) 1978, *The teaching of English in
          Japan*. Tokyo: Eichosa, 601-613.

Morsbach, Helmut
    1976   Aspects of nonverbal communication in Japan. In Larry Samovar and Richard Porter
            (eds.), 1976, *Intercultural communication: A Reader*. Belmont: Wadsworth, 240-
            259.

Müller, Brigitte
    1975   *Kōyōbun: ein Beitrag zur japanischen Sprachpolitik seit dem zweiten Weltkrieg*. Ham-
            burg: Helmut Buske.

Nagara, Susumu
    1972   *Japanese Pidgin English in Hawaii*. Honolulu: University Press of Hawaii.

Nagata, Takashi
    1984   "Phonological changes in the speech of Japanese immigrants to Hawaii". *Sophia Lin-
            guistica* 16.18-27.

Nakane, Chie
    1970   *Japanese society*. London: Weidenfield and Nicholson.

    1974   "The social system reflected in interpersonal communication". In J.L. Condon and
            Saito, M. (eds.) 1974, 124-131.

Neustupný, Jiri V.
    1974   "The modernization of the Japanese system of communication". *Language in Society*
            3.33-50.

    1978   *Poststructural approaches to language*. Tokyo: Tokyo University Press.

    1983   "Japanese language reforms". In *Kodansha Encyclopedia of Japan*, Vol.1.
            Kodansha: Tokyo, 29-32.

    1984   "Literacy and minorities: divergent perceptions". In F. Coulmas (ed.) 1984, *Linguis-
            tic minorities and literacy*. Berlin: Mouton, 115-128.

Niyekawa, Agnes M.
    1983   "Honorific language". In *Kodansha Encyclopedia of Japan*, Vol.3. Tokyo:
            Kodansha, 224-226.

Nomoto, Kikuo
    1975   "How much has been standardized over the past twenty years". In F.C. Peng (ed.)
            1975, 33-69.

Norman, Arthur
    1954   "Bamboo English". *American Speech* 30.44-8.

O'Connor, J.D. and G.F. Arnold
    1973   *Intonation of Colloquial English*. London: Longman.

Ogawa, Dennis M.
    1979   "Communication characteristics of Asian Americans in urban settings". In K.A.
            Molefi, et al. (eds.) 1979, *Handbook of intercultural communication*. London: Sage,
            321-337.

Ogasawara, Linju
1972   "Nichibei no bunka to kotoba joron". [Introduction to Japanese and American cul-
        ture and vocabulary] In Miyauchi Hideo kyōjū kanreki kinen rombunshū henshū
        īnkai (ed.) 1972, *Nichiei no kotoba to bunka*. [Japanese-English language and voc-
        abulary]. Tokyo: Sanseido, 39-56.

Ogino, Tsunao et al.
1985   "Diversity of honorific usage in Tokyo: a sociolinguistic approach based on a field sur-
        vey". In R.R. Mehrotra (ed.) 1985, 23-39.

Osawa, Akira
1977   "New tendency in Japanese reading: an oral style". *Journal of Reading* Dec. 1977,
        253-254.

Okamura-Bichard, Fumiko
1985   "Mother tongue maintenance and second language learning: a case of Japanese chil-
        dren". *Language Learning* 35:1.63-89.

O'Neill, P.G.
1966   *A programmed course in respect language in modern Japanese*. London: English Uni-
        versities Press.

Passin, Herbert
1980   *Japanese and the Japanese*. Tokyo: Kinseidō.

Peng, Fred C.
1975   "Sociolinguistic patterns of Japanese kinship behaviour". In F.C. Peng (ed.) 1975, 91-
        128.

Peng, Fred C. (ed.)
1975   *Language in Japanese society*. Tokyo: University of Tokyo Press.

Peng, F. et al. (eds.)
1981   Male/female differences in Japanese. Tokyo ICU Language Science Summer Insti-
        tute, Mitaka.

Pharr, Susan
1976   "The Japanese woman: evolving views of life and role". In L. Austin (ed.) 1976,
        Japan: The paradox of progress. New Haven: Yale University, 301-327.

Pierce, Joe
1971   "Culture, diffusion and Japlish". *Linguistics* 76.45-58.

Pike, Kenneth L.
1945   *The intonation of American English*. Ann Arbor: University of Michigan Press.

Platt, John and Heidi Weber
1980   *English in Singapore and Malaysia*. Kuala Lumpur: Oxford University Press.

Pride, John B. and David Holmes (eds.)
1972   *Sociolinguistics*. Harmondsworth: Penguin.

Prideaux, Gary
1970   *The syntax of Japanese honorifics*. The Hague: Mouton.

Prindle, Tamae K.
1972   "Japanese consanguineal kin terms". *Anthropological Linguistics* 14:5.182-195.

Pürschel, H.
1975   *Pause und Kadenz*. Tübingen: Niemeyer.

Radcliffe-Brown, Alfred Reginald
1965   *Structure and function in primitive society*. New York: Free Press.

Ramsey, Sheila J.
1981   "The kinesics of femininity in Japanese women". *Language Sciences* 3:1.104-123.

Reinecke, J.E.
1969   *Language and dialect in Hawaii*. Honolulu: University Press of Hawaii.

Richards, Jack C.
1982   "Rhetorical and communicative styles in the new varieties of English". In J.B. Pride (ed.) 1982, *New Englishes*. Rowley, Mass.: Newbury House.

Rosaldo, M.Z.
1975   "It's all uphill: the creative metaphors of Ilongot magical spells". In Mary Sanches and Ben Blount (eds.) 1975, 177-203.

Ross, John R.
1968   *Constraints on variables in syntax*. Ph.D. dissertation, MIT. Reproduced by the Indiana University Linguistics Club.

1970   "On declarative sentences". In Roderick A. Jacobs and Peter Rosenbaum (eds.) 1970, 222-272.

Rubin, J. et al. (eds.)
1977   *Language planning processes*. The Hague: Mouton.

Russel, Harriet
1981   "Second person pronouns in Japanese". *Sophia Linguistica* 8/9.116-128.

Sachs, Jacqueline, Philip Lieberman and Donna Erikson
1973   "Anatomical and cultural determinants of male and female speech". In Ralph W. Shuy and Ralph W. Fasold (eds.) 1973, *Language attutudes: Current trends and prospects*. Washington, D.C.: Georgetown University Press, 74-84.

Sadock, Jerrold M.
1974   *Toward a linguistic theory of speech acts*. New York: Academic Press.

1978   "On testing for conversational implicature". In Peter Cole (ed.) 1978, 281-297.

Saint-Jacques, Bernard
1972   "Quelques aspects du language gestuel en japonais". In J. Barrau et al. (eds.) 1972, *Langues et techniques — Nature et société, Vol.1: Approche Linguistique*. Paris: Editions Klinsieck, 391-394.

1983   "Language attitudes in contemporary Japan". *The Japan Foundation Newsletter* 11:1/2.7-14.

Saito, Horishi
1984   *Brajiru to Nihonjin* [Brazil and the Japanese]. Tokyo: Simul Press.

Sakurai, Michiko
    1984   "On the vocabulary and kinship terminology of the imperial family of Japan". *Language Sciences* 59.53-72.

Sanches, Mary
    1975   "Falling words: an analysis of a Japanese 'rakugo' performance". In M. Sanches and B.G. Blount (eds.) 1975, 269-306.

    1977a   "Language acquisition and language change: Japanese numeral classifiers". In: B.G. Blount and M. Sanches (eds.) 1977, *Sociocultural dimensions of language change*. New York: Academic Press, 51-62.

    1977b   "Reflexification and syntactic change in Japanese". *Papers in Linguistics* 10:3/4.407-466.

Sanches, Mary and Ben B. Blount (eds.)
    1975   *Sociocultural dimensions of language use*. New York: Academic Press.

Sapir, Edward
    1929   "The status of linguistics as a science". *Language* 5.207-214.

Scarcella, Robin and Joanna Brunak
    1981   "On speaking politely in a second language". *International Journal of the Sociology of Language* 27.59-75.

Scheflen, A.E.
    1972   "The significance of posture in communication systems". In John Laver and Sandy Hutcheson (eds.) 1972, 225-246.

Scherer, Klaus B.
    1979   "Personality markers in speech". In Klaus R. Scherer and Howard Giles (eds.) 1979, 147-209.

Scherer, Klaus G. and Howard Giles
    1979   *Social markers in speech*. Cambridge: Cambridge University Press.

Searle, John R.
    1971   *The philosophy of language*. Oxford: Oxford University Press.

Seward, Jack
    1968   *Japanese in action*. New York: Weatherhill.

Sherzer, Joel
    1974   "Namakke, sunmakke, kormakke: three types of Cuna speech events". In Richard Bauman and Joel Sherzer (eds.) 1974, 263-282.

Shibata, T.
    1975   "On some problems in Japanese sociolinguistics: reflection and prospects". In F.C. Peng (ed.) 1975, 159-173.

    1977   "Amae no kaiwa". *Gengo Seikatsu* 306.16.

    1985   "Sociolinguistic surveys in Japan: approaches and problems". In R.R. Mehrotra (ed.) 1985, 79-88.

Shibatani, Masayoshi (ed.)
1975   *Syntax and semantics 5: Japanese generative grammar*. New York: Academic Press.

Shimaoka, T.
1966   "A contrastive study on rhythm and intonation of English and Japanese with spectrographic analysis". *Study of Sounds* 12.347-362.

Shinoda, Eri
1981   "Donatory verbs and psychological distance in Japan". *Sophia Linguistica* 8:4.142-151.

Shohara, H.
1952   *Honorific expressions of personal attitudes in spoken Japanese*. (Occasional Papers, No.2, Center for Japanese Studies). Ann Arbor: University of Michigan Press

Smith, Philip M.
1979   "Sex markers in speech". In K.R. Scherer and H. Giles (eds.) 1979, 109-146.

Snow, Catherine et al.
1981   "The interactional origins of foreigner talk". *International Journal of the Sociology of Language* 28.81-91.

Sonoda, Koji
1975   *A descriptive study of English influence on modern Japanese*. Ph.D. dissertation, New York University.

Stalnaker, R.C.
1972   "Pragmatics". In Donald Davidson and Gilbert Harman (eds.) 1972, *Semantics of natural language*. Dordrecht: Reidel, 380-397.

Stanlaw, James
1982   "English in Japanese communicative strategies". In B.B. Kachru (ed.) 1982, 168-197.

Suzuki, Peter T.
1976   "The ethnolinguistics of Japanese Americans in the wartime camps". *Anthropological Linguistics* 18:9.416-427.

Suzuki, Takeo
1978   *Japanese and the Japanese*. Tokyo: Kodansha.

Tanaka, Masako
1977   "Kinship terminologies: The Okinawan case". In W.C. McCormack and S.A. Wurm (eds.) 1977, *Language and thought: Anthropological issues*. The Hague: Mouton, 211-226.

Tatsuki, Masāki
1982   "Devocalization in Japanese". *Doshisha Studies in English* 30.118-134.

Teeter, Karl U.
1973   "The linguistic atlas of Japan". (review). *Language* 49.506-510.

Thorne, Barrie and Nancy Henley (eds.)
1975   *Language and sex: Difference and dominance*. Rowley, Mass.: Newbury House.

Trudgill, Peter
　　1974　　*The social differentiation of English in Norwich*. Cambridge: Cambridge University
　　　　　　Press.

Ueda, Keiko
　　1974　　"Sixteen ways to avoid saying 'no' in Japan". In John C. Condon and Mitsuko Saito
　　　　　　(eds.) 1974, 185-192.

Uldall, Elizabeth
　　1964　　"Dimensions of meaning in intonation". In D. Abercrombie, D.B. Fry, P.A.D. Mac-
　　　　　　Carthy, N.C. Scott and J.L.M. Trim (eds.) 1964, *In honour of Daniel Jones*. London:
　　　　　　University Press, 271-279.

Valdman, Albert
　　1981　　"Sociolinguistic aspects of foreigner talk". *International Journal of the Sociology of
　　　　　　Language* 28.41-52.

Vogel, Ezra F.
　　1968　　*Japan's new middle class*. Berkeley: University of California Press.

Wakamori, Taro
　　1963　　"Initiation rites and young men's organizations". In Richard M. Dorson (ed.) 1963,
　　　　　　Studies in Japanese folkore. Bloomington: Indiana University Press, 291-304.

Williams, F.
　　1970　　"Language, attitudes and social change". In F. Williams (ed.) 1970, *Language and
　　　　　　poverty*. Markham: Chicago.

Waggoner, Dorothy
　　1981　　"Statistics on language use". In C.A. Ferguson and S.B. Heath (eds.) 1981, 486-515.

Wenk, Günter
　　1954　　*Japanische Phonetik*, Vol.1. Wiesbaden: Otto Harrassowitz.

Werlen, Iwar
　　1979　　"Konversationsrituale". In J. Dittman (ed.) 1979, *Arbeiten zur Konversation-
　　　　　　sanalyse*. Tübingen: Niemeyer.

　　1984　　*Ritual und Sprache*. Tübingen: Gunter Narr.

Wunderlich, Dieter
　　1971　　"Pragmatik, Sprechsituation and Deixis". *Zeitschrift für Literaturwissenschaft und
　　　　　　Linguistik* 1:2.153-190.

Wunderlich, Dieter (ed.)
　　1972　　*Linguistische Pragmatik*. Frankfurt: Athenäum.

Yamagawa, Joseph K.
　　1967　　"On dialect intelligibility in Japan". *Anthropological Linguistics* 9:1.1-17.

Yamagiwa, Joseph K.
　　1965　　"Language as an expression of Japanese culture". In John Whitney Hall and Richard
　　　　　　K. Beardsley (eds.) 1965, *Twelve doors to Japan*. Maidenhead: McGraw-Hill, 186-
　　　　　　221.

Yamamoto, Tsunetomo (transl. by Takao, Mukō)
  1980   *The Hagakure: A code to the way of the Samurai*. Tokyo: Hokuseido.

Yanagida, Kunio
  1957   *Japanese manners and customs in the Meiji Era*. Tokyo: Obunsha.

In the PRAGMATICS & BEYOND series the following monographs have been published thus far:

I:1.   *Anca M. Nemoianu*: The Boat's Gonna Leave: A Study of Children Learning a Second Language from Conversations with Other Children.
Amsterdam, 1980, vi, 116 pp. Paperbound.

I:2.   *Michael D. Fortescue*: A Discourse Production Model for 'Twenty Questions'.
Amsterdam, 1980, x, 137 pp. Paperbound.

I:3.   *Melvin Joseph Adler*: A Pragmatic Logic for Commands.
Amsterdam, 1980, viii, 131 pp. Paperbound.

I:4.   *Jef Verschueren*: On Speech Act Verbs.
Amsterdam, 1980, viii, 83 pp. Paperbound.

I:5.   *Geoffrey N. Leech*: Explorations in Semantics and Pragmatics.
Amsterdam, 1980, viii, 133 pp. Paperbound. Temporarily out of print.

I:6.   *Herman Parret*: Contexts of Understanding.
Amsterdam, 1980, viii, 109 pp. Paperbound.

I:7.   *Benoît de Cornulier*: Meaning Detachment.
Amsterdam, 1980, vi, 124 pp. Paperbound.

I:8.   *Peter Eglin*: Talk and Taxonomy: A methodological comparison of ethnosemantics and ethnomethodology with reference to terms for Canadian doctors.
Amsterdam, 1980, x, 125 pp. Paperbound.

II:1.   *John Dinsmore*: The Inheritance of Presupposition.
Amsterdam, 1981, vi, 97 pp. Paperbound.

II:2.   *Charles Travis*: The True and the False: The Domain of the Pragmatic.
Amsterdam, 1981, vi, 164 pp. Paperbound.

II:3.   *Johan Van der Auwera*: What do we talk about when we talk? Speculative grammar and the semantics and pragmatics of focus.
Amsterdam, 1981, vi, 121 pp. Paperbound.

II:4.   *Joseph F. Kess & Ronald A. Hoppe*: Ambiguity in Psycholinguistics.
Amsterdam, 1981, v, 123 pp. Paperbound.

II:5.   *Karl Sornig*: Lexical Innovation: A Study of Slang, Colloquialisms and Casual Speech.
Amsterdam, 1981, viii, 117 pp. Paperbound.

II:6.   *Knud Lambrecht*: Topic, Antitopic and Verb Agreement in Non-Standard French.
Amsterdam, 1981, vii, 113 pp. Paperbound.

II:7.   *Jan-Ola Östman*: *You Know*: A Discourse-Functional Study.
Amsterdam, 1981, viii, 91 pp. Paperbound.

II:8.   *Claude Zilberberg*: Essai sur les modalités tensives.
Amsterdam, 1981, xi, 154 pp. + 4 folding tables. Paperbound.

III:1. *Ivan Fonagy*: Situation et Signification.
Amsterdam, 1982, v, 160 pp. Paperbound.

III:2/3. *Jürgen Weissenborn and Wolfgang Klein (eds.)*: Here and There. Cross-linguistic Studies in Deixis and Demonstration.
Amsterdam, 1982. v, 296 pp. Paperbound.

III:4. *Waltraud Brennenstuhl*: Control and Ability. Towards a Biocybernetics of Language.
Amsterdam, 1982. v, 123 pp. Paperbound.